# Charles V. Catherine Dickens.

# As They Were.

## Jean Wilson

Paperback ISBN  9781780924175
ePub ISBN  9781780924182
PDF ISBN  9781780924199

Published in the UK by MX Publishing
335 Princess Park Manor, Royal Drive,
London, N11 3GX
www.mxpublishing.co.uk
Cover design by www.staunch.com

# Contents

DEDICATION .................................................................... 4

ACKNOWLEDGEMENTS .................................................. 5

A subjective point of view ..................................................... 6

Chapter One ........................................................................... 9

Chapter Two.......................................................................... 22

Chapter Three....................................................................... 33

Chapter Four ........................................................................ 48

Chapter Five......................................................................... 63

Chapter Six........................................................................... 76

Chapter Seven ...................................................................... 91

Chapter Eight ....................................................................... 107

Chapter Nine ........................................................................ 118

Chapter Ten.......................................................................... 128

Chapter Eleven..................................................................... 143

Chapter Twelve .................................................................... 156

Chapter Thirteen .................................................................. 168

# DEDICATION

This book is dedicated to Professor David Bates MA, MB, BChir, FRCP, FRCP (E) Head of Clinical Neurology at the Royal Victoria Infirmary in Newcastle-upon-Tyne.

I was presented to him as a hard to understand case, yet although specialising in a different discipline to the endocrine problem troubling me; within sixty-eighty seconds of our meeting he diagnosed a thyroid disorder, for which I have had cause to be eternally grateful.

# ACKNOWLEDGEMENTS

Quite simply, this subjective view would have no credence at all, if it weren't for the first hand account of Gladys Storey in her book, Dickens and Daughter.

Helen Thomson's letter to Mrs.Stark of 20th August, 1858 reproduced and sent to me by Cambridge University Library was also illuminating.

Miscellaneous Papers were invaluable, as was John Forster's Life of Charles Dickens Vol.2, Anonymous 1870 and the World Wide Web.

# A subjective point of view

It might be considered that it is time to propose that Dickens, in common with Shelley, Wordsworth and others, had affairs that resulted in children being born overseas who were not acknowledged.

My English teacher always said, "Charles Dickens was a great man". Had she known of his verbal abuse against his wife Catherine, she would not have spoken in this way, for his exchanges, published subsequently make very uncomfortable reading.

Dickens's verbalised assaults against his wife have a ring of madness about them – the madness he was concerned to attribute to her and it is more than shocking when considering the type of lunatic asylums he visited.

Yet Catherine, with dignity, did not retaliate. She must have been a gentle lady and he no gentleman.

To put all this into perspective it must be remembered that Queen Victoria was given an ultimatum by her son and ministers that if she did not give up her Indian manservant they would have her declared insane, so the practice of removing relatives prevailed for many years.

Returning to Charles, his later criticism of the Pre-Raphaelite painters seems to lack balance and would probably have added to the many comments at the time that he was "mad".

It is hard to understand why Dickens, in his lifetime would not try to disprove the claims reaching England from Calcutta regarding Hector Charles Bulwer Lytton Dickens being his son when he legally threatened a Scottish Editor over claims that Georgina had three children by him. His silence was uncharacteristic as I can think of no other who followed Shakespeare's dictum "Methinks thou protest too much" as faithfully.

Moving on, the fictionalised birth of a child to Ellen Ternan is my own construction but given the circumstantial evidence along with the attributed words of his daughter Kate and others, credible. Unfortunately the Paris birth records were burnt in 1871 and a search denied.

Dickens became responsible for his own family's debts which he felt compelled to settle. Thus it is difficult to believe why he would take on the Ternan family finances without some reason.

Such an extraordinary sequence of events stirs the imagination into fictionalisation.

*"When you're a married man you'll understand a good many things as you don't understand now; but whether it's worth while goin' through so much to learn so little...."*
**Charles Dickens.**

# Chapter One

C.1831.

Charles knew what he wanted - "to begin the world".

His one resolve was to be a gentleman, not a "little gentleman" as he had been while working in his uncle's factory as a child but a gentleman of the "variety" who was NEVER taken away and locked up in the Marshalsea Debtors' Prison as his father was.

His mother had instigated his employment and lodgings with the hated Mrs. Roylance while his siblings stayed with his parents and after a brief time at school had found him further work with Messrs. Ellis & Blackmore at 10/6d a week as a "writing clerk". He did not care for this and later made the change to learn a trade in his uncle's printing works while at the same time becoming a shorthand reporter in the press gallery of Doctors' Commons, where we now find him.

He has met the "real first love" of his life, Maria Beadnell.

Between St. Paul's cathedral and the murky Thames, smothering night fog enveloped Doctors' Commons. Inside the dismal building, wainscoted walls hid behind the columns supporting the roof. The Doctors swarmed in red gowns and grey wigs to surround a platform. They paid scant attention to the Presiding Judge sitting at the top of the room. Proctors wearing black gowns trimmed with white fur sat at a long table.

The Presiding Judge banged his gavel down onto the wooden table. 'I declare the Consistory Court of the Bishops' of London closed.'

The Proctors left their seats to amble around gossip mongering, yawning and in groups idling their time. One or two who had been asleep, dreamt on. Upstairs in the gallery Charles and a colleague, Thomas Potter sat in one of the reporter's boxes. They had been taking shorthand and the pads rested on their knees still.

Charles a good looking young man of nineteen, with shoulder length brown hair and a waving lock above his brow pulled out a comb and carefully arranged the last unruly strands into place before secreting it in his pocket. His dress was dandified and his waistcoat's colours arresting beside his conservatively dressed companion of a similar age. He obsessively strove to "keep up appearances" as they shrugged and pulled on their frock coats and carefully saved their pads and pencils in cavernous pockets. He slipped his hand into one of these before being propelled along with the outgoing throng of reporters. They were pushed through the narrow door.

A complaining Thomas Potter sent up a prayer, 'thank God that's over. I did think they'd go on all night. I've scarce heard such a muddled speech.'

'I have my good fellow, but the night is young and so are we for that matter.'

Outside in the London streets they dodged their way along the pavements past boot lace, Lucifer match and pickled whelk sellers.

An old woman, whom Charles had known from a child, cried out her wares. 'Grapes, tuppence a pound.

Walnuts, sixteen a penny.'

Her man added his cry. 'Get your bloaters here, three a penny.'

A small boy squatting in the alley used it as a toilet. A prostitute and her client used it for a more personal matter, not caring what the child saw. Charles and Thomas clutched their frockcoats close and Charles turned up his collar.

Thomas grumbled. 'I often wonder why they bother with all their debating.'

'I agree, it's to no avail but my wish is that it proves to be for our advancement. I get tired of their "wills, wives and wrecks".'

Thomas remained glum. 'Pity we're too late for the theatre.'

'I'm exactly of the same opinion.'

'You fancy being an actor and perhaps treading the boards.'

'I do, but I can't suppose what will become of my fancy. Something delectable?'

'You want to be near the actresses.'

'Wouldn't anyone?'

At a corner they stopped in their tracks and Potter asked. 'Is it The George or the Cheshire Cheese?'

'The oysters at the Cheese are good.' Charles's slight lisp didn't hide the fact that he was enthusiastic.

'It's the Cheshire Cheese then.'

Walking down Fleet Street a door opened in front of them and a drunken man holding a small boy by the collar threw him out into the street. 'Look after yourself, you're not my kid.'

Never looking back the sprawling boy picked his self up and limped off.

Charles and Thomas turned to one another. 'Is it "the street of ink"? Or "the street of drink"?' Charles asked.

'It looks like both.'

They turned into Wine Office Court to hear the swinging board above creak and see it spell out Ye Olde Cheshire Cheese. The smell of gin greeted them when they pushed their way into the 'men only' room. "Blue ruin" Thomas sniffed the air appreciatively.

Clamouring over knees, standing on feet and stirring up the sawdust they found seats on a settle. Charles pulled a coin out of his pocket and passed it to Thomas. 'Your turn to order at the bar but it's my turn to pay for it. I'll have their best and some oysters.'

Thomas beat his way to the counter and after a time the landlord came to him. 'The usual?' he asked.

Thomas nodded as he flipped the coins onto the trestle and the man pulled two tankards of frothing ale. Their host scraped oysters from a wooden fish box on the counter and dropped them onto small platters stacked on top of each other. Thomas made two trips back to the table without spilling too much ale. His voice was full of resentment. 'It's 2.15 p.m. I thought they'd never stop.'

'I confess, I thought so too.'

'It's incredible what goes on in Church cases. They're so sanctimonious.'

Charles mimicked the voice of the Presiding Judge. 'St. Bartholomew the Great – Jarman v. Wise.'

'Did you get it all?'

'I think so, but it will take some time to transcribe. When I've done we'll check it.'

They lapsed into silence as they did justice to a good supper then began to recall the day.

Thomas was sceptical. 'Do you think they'll ever get the Reform Bill through?'

'I very much hope so.'

Thomas quizzed. 'Are you seeing Maria tomorrow?'

'I am. She's enchanting. I think I may be in love and I believe she may be in love with me.'

'An enviable place to be, one I envy.'

They sat for some time until their yawns could not be stifled then gathered up their coats to leave and walk the dark lanes home.

'Tomorrow' came and Charles called on the Beadnells. *The Beadnells are unfailingly civil to me* he thought but he was aware that they didn't think him well enough connected to marry their daughter. Mr. and Mrs. Beadnell sat on a settee, Mrs. Beadnell holding Maria's white lapdog on her lap. Maria sat with the harp playing Home Sweet Home while her friend Mary Anne looked on. Maria's small curvaceous figure was accentuated by a raspberry coloured silk gown and black ringlets making an attractive picture.

Mrs.Beadnell    gushed.    'Wasn't    that    delightful Mr.Dickin?'

*She always calls me "Mr.Dickin".*    'It was capital Mrs.Beadnell, capital.'

The company furtively looked over at one another whilst Maria and Mary Anne giggled and allowed themselves to cast long glances at Charles but in spite of Mary Anne appropriating Maria as much as the opportunity would allow, the evening passed pleasantly until Maria ended her playing and began looking through the sheet music when Mr.Beadnell's voice rang out. 'You'll no doubt have to go now Charles. Your parents will be expecting you. Your father's making quite a name for himself in the city. Everyone's talking about him.'

*For all the wrong reasons! And he's telling me I have to go* thought Charles.

Maria stepped forward. 'I'll see Charles to the door father.'

'Be that as it may.' Mr. Beadnell got up and walked from the room as Maria escorted Charles to the front door.

A look of pique crossed Mary Anne's face.

At the front door Charles took Maria's hand. 'You know I love you.'

'Do you?'

'You know I do.'

'Perhaps you could write in my album and tell me of your love that way?'

'Is that what you want?'

'Yes, I should like that.'

'Well that's how it will be.'

Maria studied his face. 'You're such a boy.'

'I feel like a man. I have feelings like a man.'

Mary Anne joined them. 'Are you coming Maria?' She stood by her friend and Charles let himself out, realising he was not going to be allowed to be alone with his love.

He walked to Bentinck Street to find his father John snoozing at the hearth and his mother reading. Charles could not help but see that it was a cheerless place not even beginning to compare with the Beadnell's home.

His mother welcomed him. 'Did you have an agreeable evening Charles?'

'Yes Mama.'

'She's a very pretty girl and her family are so well placed. It must be very gratifying for Mrs.Beadnell to have a husband who works in a bank.'

'I agree.' Charles lifted the cheese dish cover to find it empty.

'Have you eaten Charles?' His mother asked.

'No, I was not invited to dinner, just to call.'

'I see.'

His father woke up with a start. 'Have we any rum dear?'

'No "D", we cannot get any credit.'

He grumbled. 'Money is a vexed question and always will be.'

Charles picked up one of the lit candles that threatened to go out and climbed rickety stairs to the bedroom he shared with his younger brothers. He undressed, folded his clothes and put his nightshirt on, reliving the evening as he tried to get to sleep. He ruefully remembered that it was Maria's father who had brought his visit to an end – but Maria had made sure she escorted him to the door. She had even invited him to write in her album. It must be a good sign.

He went over the hours he had spent with the Beadnells. The scene went through his mind over and over again until he succeeded in convincing himself the courtship could go favourably, if Mary Anne would keep out of the way.

Downstairs his parents sat on by the fire and Elizabeth Dickens could not hide the glee in her voice. 'The Beadnell's are doing well with their girls. Margaret is married, Anne engaged and only Maria remains. I do hope they see Charles has some prospects.'

'Quite so, but there are some things he must do for himself and this is one of them.'

Charles did strive to do everything for himself, with the result that soon after he was confiding in Fanny, his sister as they strolled along in a London park. 'I've got an audition for the theatre. It's going to be before Mathews and Charles Kemble.'

She put her arm through his. 'Charles that's wonderful, you are fortunate.' She stopped walking and studied his face. 'What did Mama and Papa say?'

'I've not taken them into my confidence yet.'

'Well I think you should. It's splendid and I shall come as your accompanist.'

'Thank you Fanny, I knew I could depend on you.'

She hugged him and they walked on happy in each other's company, Charles feeling none of the resentment he usually harboured towards Fanny and her past access to paid education by his parents.

Days later he woke to find his concerned sister standing over his bed. 'Charles whatever's the matter?'

Charles's cough made him bark abruptly. 'I'm "laid up with a terrible bad cold and an inflammation of the face".

'I'll go and get you a drink.'

He spluttered, 'I should welcome that.'

She left and returned with a mug in her hand. 'Such

bad luck. You couldn't have got a worse cold on the day of your audition. What will you do now?'

'Think on it, I always do. I shall write them of the situation and probably resume my application next season.' *Will I ever have an acting career now?*

Fanny spent time with him until he returned to work in the city. In the Mirror of Parliament's printing room a thunderous printing press filled most of the space. The printer busily set up the type while Charles, his father and uncle, John Barrow worked.

His uncle came over to his father. 'How did it go John?'

'I got it all.'

'That's what I like to hear, give them a run for their money! We can beat the Times any day of the week. I have the superior paper, always have had.'

The two men laughed and his uncle turned to him. 'And Charles, well done, you too are making your mark.'

'Thank you uncle, I'm determined it should be so.' He was going to succeed! After all, it was a time of expansion. All around London small presses were springing up, printing works were churning out vast amounts of leaflets. Magazines were becoming fashionable and newspapers were attracting a big following.

But his romantic plans were upset when Maria was sent to a finishing school in Paris and his relationship with her compounded by the fact that her friend Mary Anne implied he had paid attention to her in Maria's absence. He had imagined Mary Anne to be the jealous type and now he labelled her a troublemaker. His approaches to Maria were limited to notes only and he had just had one returned wrapped in a small loose piece of brown paper.

He read it once more in his shared bedroom before folding it away in a chest of drawers. Sometimes she had encouraged him, at others she had made him suffer.

He resolved to act differently towards women in the future. He would not be hurt or humiliated again. Shrugging his shoulders and obsessively straightening the objects lying around before tidying his hair and checking his appearance, he joined his father to go to work.

In the tiny office his uncle came to him. 'I've put in a word for you to join the Morning Chronicle.'

'I'm in your debt uncle.'

'Nonsense – you've proved yourself here, though another's gain will be my loss.'

His father looked up. 'Congratulations Charles. You're learning fast.' His father approved!

At home that evening Charles was to find out why his father had been so pleased with him at work. 'There's something I must discuss with you Charles. My creditors are determined that I'll pay one way or another. If they cannot get their money they want a pound of flesh.'

Charles stopped eating his supper. 'But father I backed your bills, they could put me in the debtors' prison too!'

His father looked aggrieved. 'They could, but it's me they're determined to detain – at least at first.'

Charles flushed.

'You will concede I had to tell you.'

His father had acquainted him of the facts only moments before a rap on the front door made them all jump.

When the door stood open he saw two men on the step who demanded of his father without ceremony. 'Are you John Dickens?'

'I am he.'

'We're arresting you for non payment of a debt. It's the detention house for you.'

Their father was taken away once again. When he had gone his mother wrung her hands. 'You will look to your father's affairs Charles?'

'I am made destitute by father's indiscretions.'

'We are disgraced; my father will not advance us money. What's to be done Charles? What's to be done?'

The thoughts went around in Charles's head. *Yet again the prison beckons to me.* 'I'll consult my friends Mitton and Beard and see if they will advance the sum, but first there is bed, I must work tomorrow.'

Next morning he left for the Mirror of Parliament press and entered the printing room. His uncle glanced around. 'Where's your father.'

'I'm afraid he's indisposed Sir.' Charles attempted to cover for his missing parent.

His uncle looked sceptical. 'Really, what's wrong with him?'

'His old trouble; it is a urinary inconvenience, Sir.'

'I'm sorry to hear it. Perhaps he'll be in tomorrow?'

'I cannot say Sir.' Charles bent down over his shorthand pad.

That night on his way home he passed the same old man and woman he always saw. The old man plied his wares. 'Get your fish. A penny 'ill feed y'u all, three a penny.' The

19

old woman offered him a walnut which he accepted.

It took a little time before Charles was ready to go to the Marshalsea Debtors' Prison and gain admittance to the very dimly lit lodge. He knew the building. He'd visited his father there since he was a boy.

A gaoler sat at a table. 'Yes?'

'You have my father Sir, John Dickens and I'm here to pay his debt.'

The gaoler shuffled the papers in front of him until he found the one he needed. Then he ordered the gaoler standing behind him. 'Get Dickens.' He scrutinised Charles. 'Have you the money?'

'Yes Sir.' Charles put his hand in his pocket and drew out coins which he placed on the table in front of the man. It was counted, his father brought into the room and Charles given a receipt for the sum.

Together Charles and his father made their escape and walked briskly away from the prison. Children seeing them come out of the prison gates chanted;

'I spy blue,

I spy black,

I spy a peeler in a shiny hat.'

In passing the many coffee houses, his father slowed his pace and began a speech. 'Once again Charles.....'

Charles walked off without listening.

His father stood momentarily watching his son then went straight home to be greeted by an effusive wife. 'Oh "D" we're so glad your here.'

'I'm glad to be here my dear, there's really no place like home.'

'Something does always turn up.'

When Charles felt he could go back he entered a house in darkness. In bed that night he resolved to leave and guessed he would have no difficulty in persuading fourteen year old Fred to go with him.

Soon after he sounded out his idea to his sibling and within days his brother stuffed his clothes into a canvas bag while Charles meticulously folded his and put them on top. They went downstairs to their waiting parents. Their father sat reading the paper and did not put it down. Their mother was tearful. 'Your big adventure Charles.'

'Yes Ma'am.'

She went to Fred and put her arm around him. 'Look after him.' She appealed to Charles.

John Dickens put his paper down in exasperation. 'Tut-tut my dear, they'll look after each other.'

Charles addressed his father, '"Sir we are your responsibilities, you are not ours. I must pay £35 for rent in advance for Furnivals Inn where we are now going. I have few dishes and no carpets or curtains. What's more things cannot continue as they are and Mama and the children must be found cheaper lodgings. You must look to your own affairs".'

John Dickens glared at Charles as Elizabeth kissed both of her sons on their forehead.

Charles picked up the canvas bag. 'We will see you soon Ma'am;' and they left for their new chambers. He'd been away from the family when he was a small boy but this time he was grown and there was Fred. It wasn't a new situation.

# Chapter Two

In his job at the Morning Chronicle office Charles met new people from the publishing world. John Black was his boss and George Hogarth acted as music and drama critic. He knew Thomas Beard a fellow reporter.

George Hogarth came over to him. 'And how are you settling in?'

'Very well Sir. It is convivial work.'

'We're glad you find it so, indeed find us so. How are the sketches coming on?'

'I'm working on them Sir, I've done five slips and they're working out well.'

'Good, good that couldn't be better. Would you care to come around to the house and discuss them this evening? Mrs. Hogarth will put some supper on.'

Charles suddenly felt he'd been noticed. He'd never had an invitation to dine before. 'I'll be punctual Sir.'

George Hogarth disappeared and Thomas Beard came over to Charles. 'I think Hogarth's impressed with you.'

'I'm trying to make impressions.'

'You will. Hogarth's impressed.'

The day passed and Charles seemed to attract as much ink to himself as he had collected blacking to his clothes while working in his uncle's factory as a "little gentleman" yet nothing could dampen his spirits and anticipation as he hurried through the back streets to Furnivals Inn. The tiny building comprised a frugal room and an adjoining bedroom; underneath them they had a cellar. He greeted his brother, 'I'm out this evening Fred.'

'I'll be alright.'

'Sure? You can read my books if you wish.'

'I may go to see Mama and Papa.'

'Capital, can I ask you to put a note in Chapman and Hall's door for me, on the way?'

Fred nodded. 'I know where they are. They're the publishers.'

'Good man.' Charles patted his hair in front of the mirror, straightened his waistcoat and adjusted his cravat. He had a spring in his step as he made his way to the Hogarth home through lanes with rivers of sewage running down the middle. Where the alleys were blocked by excrement he had to pick his way around the piss puddles. The smallest of children played in the mess while the adults chin wagged and stood in huddles together, turning a blind eye to the deviation around them.

York Place, his destination in Fulham Road turned out to be a much grander establishment than he'd ever been inside. It was comfortably furnished but always, as Charles was to find out, tended to untidiness. Mrs. Hogarth, an excitable lady, presided over her brood of four girls, nineteen year old Catherine and a shy fourteen year old Mary sitting next to seven year old Georgina. Toddler Helen played around the floor. The older girls were looking through sheet music scores together.

George Hogarth took Charles over to one side. 'You know I'm to be Editor of the Evening Chronicle?'

Charles extended his hand to his host who shook it vigorously. 'That's wonderful news Sir.'

'Yes I'm looking forward to it. But I've a task for you too. Your sketches – could you do them for the Evening Chronicle?'

It took seconds for Charles to consider. 'I would expect *"some* additional remuneration" Sir.'

'I'm sure that could be accommodated. Would another two guineas be an agreeable sum?'

'That would be admirable Sir.'

'I think we can consider it done. Make yourself comfortable.'

'Thank you Sir. You will not find me an idler.'

'I'm certain I shan't.' They shook hands.

The girls finished arranging the music in piles and George Hogarth took up a position in front of the fireplace, reached for his instrument and played an air. While the music filled the room Charles glanced at Catherine, who returned his look. He saw her youthfulness, beautiful blue eyes, framed by glossy brunette hair and warm smile. At the end of the recital the girls busied themselves bringing refreshments in to lie on the table.

Mrs. Hogarth called to him. 'Do help yourself Charles. May I call you Charles?'

'Yes please do Ma'am, that's my name.'

Catherine stood by the table and Mrs.Hogarth gave Charles a plate. He chose from an array of food, then he and Catherine again studied each other.

'You're Catherine?' He asked her.

'Yes.'

Charles noted her soft slightly Scottish burr. It sounded charming. He had never heard anything quite like it in cockney

24

London. 'I shall call you Kate.'

She said nothing and returned to her sisters. Charles was about to eat when he was waylaid by his host. 'Do you think the ideas will come?'

'I'm sure they will. Does "Sketches of London" sound right?'

'Admirable, I leave it in your capable hands.'

'Thank you Sir. I won't let you down.'

Next morning in the office John Black sought Charles out. As he talked Thomas Beard perched on a tall stool nearby; working on an overdue article for the next day's paper.

'Charles how does a trip to Devon appeal?'

'Whatever it is you require.'

'Lord John Russell's parliamentary contest has to be covered. Take Beard with you.'

Their boss left the room and Charles groaned. 'Well I hope they get better horses this time. The last time they couldn't do over fifteen miles an hour.'

'I hope so. I've never seen such half dead nags.'

George Hogarth put his head around the door. 'Charles when you're free, call over one evening.'

'Thank you Sir.'

Charles and Thomas laboured tirelessly all day and well into the night.

The following day, just after dawn outside the Morning Chronicle, a battered stage coach drew up. The driver 'Devon' so named because he hailed from those parts, got down and gave the front wheel a few whacks with a hammer which he kept ready in his pocket. Whatever he intended seemed to have been achieved because he stowed his weapon on the bench from where he would steer the coach on the journey. The postboy slouched asleep on the back in a drunken stupor.

Charles and Thomas Beard came out of the works in time to see 'Devon' give the postillion a shove to push him off his perch. The lad recovered enough to stow away their canvas bags as Charles and Thomas climbed in. There was a cursory glance from 'Devon' and they were ready. Their driver climbed on board and took hold of the reigns.

The postboy blew on a horn hanging from his neck. 'All aboard, 'Devon'.' He piped up in his cockney voice.

'Devon' whipped the team of four horses and they clattered off, throwing Charles and Thomas from side to side. They didn't get very far before the front wheel came off and rolled away into the grass. The coach chassis grounded itself onto the earthen road.

'Not again, that bloody wheel.' 'Devon' found relief in the expletive.

Charles listening to the coachman realised with distaste that the man did not have the vocabulary to express himself and commented to Thomas, 'there's no place for bad language in a public place.'

All disembarking, Charles and Thomas looked around to find something to sit on.

'Devon' ordered his postillion 'go and find another wheel and be quick about it.'

The lad had difficulty in picking up the wheel and no-one helped as he staggered away. It took hours before he returned carrying a wheel with another young apprentice. The coachman had to pay up before the wooden hub was thumped into its place. Weary miles gave way to an even more wearing political meeting.

When they eventually got back to London the next day John Black lost no time in searching them out. 'How did it go?'

Charles and Thomas exchanged looks. 'It was an uncomfortable journey Sir. We lost a wheel.' Charles explained.

Thomas went further. 'And just the same when we got there; the rain was never ending and I had to hold a handkerchief over the notebook as Charles took it down.'

'Do you think you got it?'

'I'm pretty sure it will all be there when we get it transcribed.' Charles didn't hide his confidence.

'I knew you could do it. We'll beat the Times men.' John Black patted them both on the back and went to his own desk.

George Hogarth had been listening and put his coat on to leave. He directed his gaze in Charles's direction. 'If you get finished come over to the house for supper.'

'Thank you Sir.'

Hogarth left and Charles voiced his misgivings. 'This won't get done in time to go for supper.'

'I didn't like to say so.' Thomas agreed.

Hours later when the small press was in darkness, Charles and Thomas let themselves out and locked the door. 'What do you think?' Charles was uncertain.

'I know what I think. I'm away to my bed and if I were you I would do the same.'

Charles wavered. 'I might just drop by and tell him it's finished.'

They shook hands and parted, Charles nearly falling over the children huddled over a steam vent of the next door newspaper press. He made his way to York Place. *Will I see Catherine?* He wondered.

The door was opened by a young maidservant.

'Are the Hogarths at home?'

'Yes Sir, come in.'

Charles was shown into the drawing room where the family were. George Hogarth stood up to greet him. 'Where's Thomas?'

'He was tired Sir and thought he should go to his bed but he sends his apologies. The work has gone to press.'

'Well done, come and sit down.'

His host called over to the maidservant who was clearing the food away. 'Bring a tray for Charles.'

'There's no need, I'll dine when I get home.' He wondered if there would be anything in the larder.

'Nonsense.'

Mrs. Hogarth beckoned him and he sat down next to her. 'You must be famished after your journey.'

'A little: Fate conspired against us; the wheel came off the stagecoach.'

Mrs. Hogarth gasped. 'Well I hope we can recompense you in some measure with a good supper. Here it comes now.'

Charles was presented with a laden tray at the table and Catherine and Mary sang a duet. When he finished his supper and Mary sang alone he went to Catherine. 'May I?'

'Of course, sit down.'

Charles seated himself comfortably and looked around admiringly. 'You have a very comfortable home here.'

'Yes Papa and Mama make us very contented.'

'That's how it should be.'

'Is it not always so?'

'I wouldn't think it could be; life's so diverse is it not?'

'Of course.'

'It's pleasant coming here.'

'It's pleasant having you.'

'I appreciate your welcome. May I walk with you sometime?'

'I should like that.'

'I shall ask your father.' He immediately crossed the room to his host. 'May I take Catherine out to walk sometime soon?'

'Yes Charles you can, I know you will take care of her. Mary will chaperone.'

'Thank you Sir.' His life seemed to be taking a different direction. Catherine appeared very different from Maria. Maria had been flirtatious, whereas Catherine appeared "placid" and "easy going". She appeared to have a "sweet-natured" disposition and would perhaps be a lot more malleable than Maria Beadnell. He was able to talk to her more openly than he had ever done to Maria.

He began to fit into York Place as a suitor to Catherine. He gained confidence being accepted for what he could do not his father's past background. One bright day his sense of theatre would not be denied and he decided to play a prank. He arrived at York Place dressed as a sailor. Seeing the drawing room window partly open he lifted the sash and jumped into the room to dance a sailor's hornpipe. Mrs.Hogarth was startled but the family were very gracious. He then leapt through the window as he had arrived, changed into everyday clothes and knocked on the front door to re-enter, shake hands all around and enjoy the joke.

Scarlet fever visited London and Catherine and her mother were both taken ill. Charles sent Fred with a jar of blackcurrant jam to ease Catherine's throat. He wrote her "Should you not be well, I must see you and will not be prevented". When he had a cold or was busy he told her, "You may be disappointed; - I would rather you would – at not seeing me; but you cannot feel vexed at my doing my best with the stake I have to play for – you and a home for both of us".

They spent much of their courting time in the park. Being a green place and not involving expenditure, it commended itself. Another favoured spot was the riverbank, scene of many of Charles's childhood escapades. With Catherine he would search out somewhere to sit and watch the panorama of the river, if the stench wasn't too pungent. One day on such an outing, Mary wandered off a little distance and Charles began what would turn out to be his proposal. 'And do you care for London?'

'I do, but I like Edinburgh and we still have people there, so we enjoy both cities. We like the castles in each place – I should like to live in a castle.'

'I wouldn't care for a castle. I would want some arrangement that was more comfortable, a family home – to set up with someone of my choice.' He looked at Catherine and noted her shyness. 'How wonderful it would be to find a person to share such a place.' Charles offered his arm to Catherine and she took it. 'I call you Kate but I shall call you many pet names. I always give pet names to my family.'

'But I'm not your family.'

'Would you like to be?'

'Yes.'

'Then I shall ask your father.'

'I scarcely know you.'

'Then you've a lifetime to find me out.' He hesitatingly kissed her.

'When will you ask Papa?'

'There's no time like the present. ' It had been easy, he hadn't realised it would be.

Mary drifted back to make their way home and Charles was a little disconcerted to see when they arrived that all the family were present in the drawing room. For an instant he wondered if he had judged his timing correctly.

It was going to be a lot harder now! He went straight to George Hogarth. 'Sir I've something to ask of you. Will you give me Catherine's hand in marriage?'

George Hogarth hesitated for only a moment. 'Most assuredly:' He looked at his wife for confirmation. 'That's so, isn't it?'

'Yes George, how exciting.' Mrs. Hogarth came over to Catherine with her arms outstretched to embrace her. 'How lovely my dear.' She extended her hand to Charles. 'This is all delightful.'

George kissed his daughter and shook Charles by the hand. 'Congratulations Charles.'

Mary came forward. 'Isn't it agreeable that Charles is to be one of the family?'

'It is indeed.' Her father agreed.

31

Charles was considered as almost family and it was his good fortune to be taken under George Hogarth's wing. It was a time of introductions and swift change for him. His circle of acquaintances and colleagues grew and he found he had more than enough people to spend time with.

He had never been so settled. Furnivals Inn was a home to Fred and himself. For the first time he was in charge of his life.

# Chapter Three

As was his custom, Charles sat with Thomas in Ye Olde Cheshire Cheese. The 'men only' room being tiny and packed was full of smoke and it wasn't easy to see distinctly the people in the room. The door opened and John Macrone, a successful publisher, looked over heads. When he saw Charles he came over. 'Just the fellow I was hoping to see. I've got an idea for an enterprise Dickens. How about reprinting some of your stories and sketches in volume form? I would buy the copyright – say £100? Cruikshank has agreed to illustrate for us.'

'What can I say? Cruikshank is a good artist.'

'The best; he can be difficult at times, but on the whole he is a good man. Think it over and we'll discuss the title, both your names on it of course.'

Charles couldn't sleep in the small cramped bed with Fred that night. He was being sought out. People wanted him to write. It was exactly what he wanted. He was distancing himself from any association with a debtors' prison, but as the project neared completion a rift developed between himself and Cruikshank over the work. For Charles it was a new excursion into publishing and he found it a torturous business. His skills lay in writing, not in diplomacy and publishing agreements.

Yet over months his circumstances continued to alter and improve until one day there was a ring at the bell. Charles went to answer and found an expensively dressed man standing in the street. Charles knew him as William Hall, a partner in a new publishing firm along with Thomas Chapman.

His caller spoke 'I'm William Hall. I believe we have met briefly some time ago and you dropped a note through our door.'

'Yes that's true, please come in.' Charles showed him into the parlour. 'Make yourself comfortable.'

'Thank you. My errand is simple. We're looking for someone to write the 'script for Seymour's drawings. The pay is nine guineas a sheet and we need one and a half sheets a month. What do you say?'

'I say it sounds capital. I accept.'

'Good, good, I hear you're with the Morning Chronicle. They run a tight ship.'

'They do Sir and I'm pleased to be on board.'

'Good, good.' They shook hands and William Hall got up to leave. 'We'll be in touch.'

'"Capital".'

Charles showed him out and having business to attend to briskly set off through the London lanes to come back at dusk when his affairs were in order. He let himself into a darkened house and joined Fred in bed. 'An adventure is to be ours, we're to move to bigger quarters, only a step away but you'll agree it will be more commodious than here when we're installed.' Fred snuffled and didn't respond, yet days later he was eager enough to carry with his brother, their few possessions to a nearby property. Charles looked out of the window. 'Didn't I say it was more commodious? It will suit our purpose well.'

In York Place Catherine was beginning to understand she might not see as much of Charles as she thought. She sat reading a letter from him when Mary came in.

'Is it a letter from dear Charles?'

'Yes and he's been given more work by a firm of publishers, there's more money to be earned.'

'Oh Catherine I'm so pleased for you both.'

'He can't come today.' There was no hiding the despondency in her voice.

The realisation that there might not be a lot of time for her in Charles's life was beginning to take hold even as they chatted and when Mary left she read on. 'I'm writing "to remind you of my repeated and solemn assurance of entertaining for you a love which nothing can lessen – an affection which no alteration of time or circumstance can ever abate".'

She couldn't ask for more, could she?

One of Charles's passions was theatre and he decided to treat himself. He paid his entrance money and threaded his way into the pit with its backless seats. Sawdust had been scattered over the floor a long time ago and candlelight and rancid oil lamps burned throughout the performance. The atmosphere was raucous among an audience of adults, children and undesirables and Charles sat observing the goings on with not a little interest.

A buxom girl came down the aisle with a tray of oranges hanging from a chord around her neck. A toothless man pulled her down onto his knee but she shrugged him off and continued. A mariner who had been watching took hold of the girl's arm as she passed. 'Now then, you're selling more than oranges, how about if I wait for you outside after this?'

'Sailor you'll have a good time, I'll make you shiver

your timbers.'

The mariner slapped her bottom and she minced away.

After the theatre on the floor by the public, the Master of Ceremonies came onto the stage. 'Citizens it is with great pleasure we present to you this evening for your delectation – Othello.'

The audience cheered, jeered and stamped their feet on the once saw dusted floor and it took some little time for them to settle down. A crudely painted backcloth painted as a street scene in Venice dropped crazily into its place. Two actors made their debut.

Roderigo began. "'Tush….".'never tell me, I take it much unkindly………".'

Charles sat enthralled throughout the evening then as usual took his supper in Ye Olde Cheshire Cheese. He was thinking of leaving when William Hall and Thomas Chapman came in. They sat down to talk and Charles speculated. 'I'm thinking of a name for the text we're working on, I see the name and words first and then the illustrator fitting his work to mine.'

Hall didn't hide his irritation. 'You know that's not the way it's done. It's Seymour's drawings first and you add your words to his drawings.'

'That's not the way I work.'

'Well I'll put it to him, but he won't be happy.'

There was a prickly silence.

Charles stood up 'there's work to do.'

'At this hour?' Hall queried.

'Any hour is good enough. I'll bid you goodnight.'

Both men nodded.

As he wound his way home Charles reflected he had spent less time in the hostelry than he usually did. He felt a pang of misgiving – it wasn't going to be easy dealing with third parties. Unforeseen obstacles were getting in the way.

A part of his life that seemed more certain was the Hogarths. He became a frequent visitor to York Place yet Catherine knew very little about his background. On one of their by now usual excursions in the park Catherine waited her chance and when Mary talked to a passing friend she tested Charles. 'When will I meet your parents?'

'I cannot say they are moving home at the moment.' He hesitated. 'I have a confession to make. My parents have fallen on "hard times" and do not enjoy the same standards as yours do. You will have seen I am working all the hours I can and my dearest love I cannot promise you a great deal at present but I hope this will all change and we'll be solvent as others are.'

'Is that why we cannot go to the theatre?'

'Yes that's so. I love such things as you do but they're not within my remit at the moment.'

'I can wait for things to change as long as you make time for me after we're married. Promise me?'

'I can't be held to account. I want the name Dickens to be held in esteem.'

'Papa's name is held in esteem and he makes time for us.'

'Do not concern yourself so.'

When he got home that evening he straightened his chair and items on his desk. He attended to his hair in front of the mirror and seated himself, drew paper and a pen to him

37

and wrote.

Dearest Kate,

"Forgive me but I can't see you in the time before we are married. I have much to do and little time to do it. The work will be no joke, but the emolument is too tempting to resist".

Yours, Charles.

He read it, put it into an envelope and addressed it.

The following evening inside the smog of Ye Olde Cheshire Cheese he and Thomas Beard sat drinking in the 'men only' room. Charles had a question for his colleague. 'I've been meaning to ask you something.'

'Go ahead.'

'George Hogarth's daughter has said she will marry me and I hoped you would be my best man.'

'Delighted, when is it to be?'

'2nd April, at St.Luke's.'

'I'll check and see if I'm free. I trust I am.'

Before the wedding the engaged couple had their first quarrel. A newspaper reporter, known to the Hogarth family had seen Charles at the theatre and mentioned the fact to George Hogarth. When Catherine learnt of this she was upset because Charles had said his insolvency prevented them from going to the theatre as a couple. She brought up the matter and his reaction was to write her saying she had a "sudden and uncalled for coldness" and telling her "a sudden inflexible obstinacy would not be tolerated". 'She must apologise.'

She did so, allowing the wedding to go ahead.

2nd April, 1836.

St.Luke's Church, Chelsea was the setting of their very private wedding. On one side of the church were the Hogarths and the other, the Dickens family. Henry Burnett who later married Fanny, Charles's sister was present. Thomas Beard acted as best man and after the ceremony Catherine and Charles were taken in a carriage to York Place. Charles helped his bride down from the carriage and up the front steps. In the dining room a wedding breakfast had been laid out and there were presents to open. Charles put a wrapped parcel into Catherine's hands. Inside it was a sandalwood box inlaid with ivory. He spoke confidentially, 'for you my "missus".'

'Is that my new name Charles?'

'It is Kate and I've many more to come.' He kissed his bride.

Chalk, Kent.

At last the stagecoach stopped and Charles paid the driver. The coach rattled off into the night as Charles opened the door and carried Catherine over the threshold, putting her down they looked around the lower floor of the cottage. 'I think an early night is in order, is it not?'

'Yes kind Sir.'

They went up the stairs together. Charles lit a candle and they undressed on either side of the bed. He put on his nightshirt and she her nightgown. They lay down very close to one another and Charles spoke softly, 'the day went well. I'm content.'

She looked up into his face, 'content?'

'Yes I have what is necessary. I've secured a home and I have you. We will have a family. I'll do what I set out to do, I'll write to ensure we are not without. When I was small my father and I used to walk past a very large house, they call it

Gad's Hill and he often said to me "if you were to be persevering and were to work hard, you might some day come to live in it". I've not forgotten and perhaps one day it will be so if things go as I intend. Your duty will be to care for our children and I will do my part towards bringing them into the world.' He tentatively took her into his arms.........

Early next morning Charles was up re-arranging furniture. His placing of each piece was meticulous. With difficulty he brought a desk standing in a dark corner to underneath a window. With care he arranged the pens, ink and paper that he had brought with him.

Catherine came slowly down the stairs rubbing her eyes. 'What are you doing?'

'I always work in the daylight. I must have everything just so.'

A nonplussed Catherine said nothing.

Later as they strolled along the beach she put her arm through his and Charles warned her. 'You must not be "cos" with me my dear if I do a little writing while we are here, I have much work to get through if I'm to make my way and provide for us.'

Catherine's answer was hesitant. 'But I get lonely Charles.'

'I know you do but you must learn to be patient.'

'I'll try.'

'When we get back to London you can ask Mary to come to stay for company. In fact I will ask your father if she may come.'

She dropped her arm from his. Again she did not want to say what was in her head, but the thoughts spun around. 'Do

40

you love me?'

'Such a question, we are married. Aren't you my "missus"?'

'Charles if our feelings for each other were to ever change would you tell me?'

'Most certainly I would but they are not likely too.' He looked at her crestfallen face. 'Have we a pact then? We tell each other if it should happen?'

'Yes Charles.' She slipped her arm back through his.

'Silly goose.' He patted her hand.

Back in London Charles and Catherine rejoined Frank at Furnivals Inn. They hosted one of their first dinner parties. 'Are we ready?' Charles asked Catherine.

'Yes the wine is decanted.' She checked the glasses and stoppered bottle on a tray.

'It's important to impress Seymour and Chapman and Hall for that matter. I've asked Seymour to change one of the illustrations, I don't think he'll take it lightly but we'll see. It's no easy task taking into account the needs of illustrators.'

The visitors arrived and after the meal Catherine left the room. Charles and Seymour now regarded each other with open mutual hostility.

Seymour's exasperation was evident. 'We seem to have difficulties.'

'Difficulties?' Charles faced him out.

'Yes difficulties. You want to change my illustrations and leave your captions. Every other writer accepts that the writer adds words to the illustrator's work, not the other way around.'

'That's not the way I work. I cannot see the method

41

being a success.' Charles quickly combed his hair.

'I had heard you were difficult.'

'We hold conflicting views.'

The evening proved fraught, Seymour left in a temper and two days later his suicide was reported. Catherine sat sewing and Charles looked up from his newspaper, tapping it with his hand. 'Seymour has killed himself. I hope my critics will not infer that I had any hand in the affair – after all I only asked him to work differently. The man is clearly unbalanced.'

'Oh no! What a dreadful thing to happen.'

'It is indeed, we've only printed the first edition and I don't know what will be done.'

'His poor wife must be heartbroken.'

'Someone else will have to be found to do the illustrations, but I can't conceive who.' He paused to reveal what had been on his mind for some days. 'There's something I've been meaning to say. I'm sick of reporting. I'm tired of careering around in stage coaches. I would much rather just write and be accountable to myself.'

'Can you afford to do that Charles?'

'Just leave that to me. I will look to my affairs and you must look to yours.'

She wondered at the hostility in his voice. Did he mean to snub her or was she being ultra sensitive? It seemed best not to question his actions. She tried to banish the growing negative thoughts about her marriage.

Charles spent a great deal of time away from Catherine. He sat with his contemporaries in Ye Olde Cheshire Cheese. The talk revolved on Seymour and the need to get another illustrator.

Thomas Chapman hoped he had the solution. 'I think the most acceptable idea yet is that Dickens writes an extra half a sheet each month and the illustrations be reduced. Has anyone any ideas who we can get?'

'I know a good man. I could have a word with him and see if he's interested.' Charles's lisp was detectable.

Thomas Chapman broke in. 'Do that Dickens, we need to find someone soon. Who is it?'

'It's Hablot Knight Browne – I've seen his work.'

'Is it good?'

'Yes.'

'When can you see him?' Hall had a troubled look on his face.

'I can see him tomorrow.'

'Good man, we need this business resolved.' Hall was pacified.

Charles recognised his literary endeavours were somewhat compromised but believed his domestic arrangements were settled. Mary was often present in his married home, Furnival's Inn. She hero worshipped him and he found it satisfying that a fresh young miss appreciated his worth. He actively encouraged her whereas Catherine on the other hand tended to be clinging and he discouraged this.

On a misty day Mary shopped with her mother. She and Mrs.Hogarth stood looking in The Old Curiosity Shop's bowed window. 'I'll go inside and enquire whether they have a copper kettle.' Mrs.Hogarth pushed the door open and stepped on to a wooden planked, creaking floor.

The bell above the architrave rang and they were greeted by Mr.Honor who fussed over his stock re-arranging it on the dusty shelves. 'What can I show you Madam?'

'Have you a copper kettle?'

'Most certainly I have.' He went to a table, picked up a copper kettle and dusted it with his arm. 'This will answer.' He put the kettle into Mrs. Hogarth's hands.

She turned it around. 'How much are you asking?'

'Two pounds Madam.'

'It seems a great deal of money.'

'Madam it is a great deal of kettle.'

'I suppose so.' She turned the kettle upside down.

Mr.Honor took it from her and set it on the counter. 'It has a strong base.'

Mrs. Hogarth hesitated. 'I'll take it.' She carefully took two pounds from her purse and gave it to the shopkeeper.

'I'll wrap it Ma'am.' He clumsily wrapped the kettle in old newsprint.

Meanwhile Mary moved along scrutinising the shelves and picking up a small pewter inkwell, examined it. 'Mother can I buy this for Charles? He's a writer and belongs to our family. I think he might like to have it.'

'I'm sure he will. I dare say there's no harm in it, yes you may.'

'How much is the inkwell.' Mary enquired of Mr.Honor.

'Ten shillings Miss.'

She looked disappointed.

'Go on then, seven shillings and sixpence.'

Mary took coins from her purse and handed them to him.

'I'll wrap it for you.' He fastened newsprint around the

inkwell and gave it to her. Mary followed Mrs. Hogarth from the shop as the bell above the door tinkled.

The Hogarths often entertained the newly weds at York Place. One evening they all sat around the table finishing dinner. As often happened the subject turned to work. Charles trusted his father-in-law's judgement. 'I brought some proofs for you to look at George.'

'Certainly, I'll look at them as soon as I'm able.' He poured port into Charles's glass. 'And how is the house hunting going? Have you seen anything suitable?'

'Not yet but I mean to begin in earnest soon. There's one thing I'm short of and that's time, time is passing. I am endeavouring to deal a "sledge hammer blow" at my writing and that brings me to another matter. Is it possible that Mary could live with us and be companion to Kate? She gets lonely when the pressure of work keeps me from her.'

George Hogarth looked at his wife, who nodded her agreement. 'If she so wishes.'

Around the dinner table they all turned to Mary who coyly replied. 'I should like that.'

A gratified Charles pronounced. 'It will be a splendid arrangement.'

Catherine had no part in the conversation. Charles had mentioned the possibility of having Mary live with them but she had not expected it to happen without any further discussion. She wanted to be on her own with Charles. They were newly married! Her heart sank further as her father artlessly began to talk.

'Mary has become quite a critic of yours Charles and has bought you an inkwell.' He directed Mary. 'You may bring it.'

Mary got up and crossed to the sideboard where her small parcel lay. She brought it over to Charles who took it from her to open it. 'It's very fine, I'll use it always. You will see me do so as you and Kate are to keep company.'

Catherine's young sister became one of a threesome in Furnival's Inn and then of course there was Fred, making four in the cramped house. Catherine began to feel resentful. She never had Charles to herself! It was her tangible concern.

Within weeks a day came when Charles came home a lot later than usual, ran his fingers through his hair and hung up his coat on a hook on the hallstand shouting out. 'My last day over for the Chronicle.'

Catherine came out from the drawing room. 'Charles, that's wonderful.'

'It is my "missus". Come we will join Mary.'

'John has arrived.'

'Capital, we'll have some merriment.'

They went into the drawing room where Mary and John Forster, Charles's newly discovered mentor were present, the two had been born in the same year and had a great deal in common. Charles's spirits boiled over and he twirled Mary around. 'My last day is over. Let's celebrate. I shall sing you The Dog's Meat Man.' He sang '"EVERY evening he was seen……..".' Coming to the end he waited. 'How was that?' He searched Forster's face.

'Admirable Charles but I'm on my way to see Chapman and Hall. I just called in.' Forster made his excuses.

'Nonsense, you must have a brandy and water while I regale you with impersonations of Mathews.'

'Our associates will be waiting.'

'Be that as it may you must hear one more song before you go. It will be The Prentice to his Mistress.' Charles postured and sang. '"Come, come, Miss Prissy, make it up and we will lovers be".' He ended his recital and his audience clapped their hands.

Mary gasped. 'You were wonderful Charles.'

The singing went on and an agreeable evening was spent. Charles for the most part doing the singing and posturing; he was in his element.

Catherine slept late next morning and when she made her way to the room where Charles wrote she heard Charles affirming through the open door. 'Mary my dear, you're not intruding, never think that.'

Mary came out of the room and saw Catherine. 'I'm going to have breakfast.' She quickly disappeared.

Catherine entered Charles's writing room. He looked up. 'Catherine, you know I don't like to be disturbed when I write.'

She withdrew, remembering she initially had fewer reservations at having her sister with them but now she was beginning to feel very differently. She could not deny to herself that Charles always showed regard for Mary's feelings while he lost patience with herself.

# Chapter Four

Catherine found her position in the "little" house was increasingly to accommodate the wishes of those beneath its small roof. Charles needs having the most importance. She felt like an outsider and when Charles un-expectantly came to the bedroom he found her sitting on a chair, she had been sick and held a towel. He stood at the door, 'arc you indisposed?'

'I think I'm to have a child.'

'So soon?'

He went to her and lifted her to her feet. 'Come, you'll need to rest and I will have to use my pen even more to provide for three of us.' He saw her into bed and vanished to begin his writing.

He was driven by the need to find a larger home for their growing numbers and Catherine accompanied him at first but scarcely any time went by before her coming confinement meant she could not keep up his pace on house hunting trips and so Charles continued his search, with Mary as his second.

It occurred to Catherine that Charles had brought Mary into their home as her companion but she was often on her own and insecurity surfaced.

In the New Year of 1837 Charles arranged to take Mary on a shopping expedition. She held his arm as they strolled through the streets of London looking at furniture. They were drawn to one shop and Charles asked her, 'should we go in? I've long wished to buy you a desk for your room.' He held the door open and the desk was bought for her.

Days later he and Mary "wandered up and down

Holborn and the streets about, for hours, looking after a little table for Catherine's bedroom". Inside the premises the shopkeeper enquired. 'What can I show you Sir?'

'I'm interested in the small table in the window.'

'Does Madam think it pleasing?'

'I'm sure it is, but it's not for me, it's for my sister.'

'I beg your pardon. I thought you were wed.'

Mary blushed and Charles ignored the man's mistake. 'What is the price?'

'To you, ten pounds, Sir.'

'Is that your best price?'

'It is.'

'Very well, please rap it.'

Charles offered Mary his arm and she took it leaving the shop. He whispered, 'we have strolled for hours. I'm so glad you are keeping house for me, "I shall never be so happy again….. Never, if I roll in wealth and fame".'

They returned back to Furnival's Inn and Charles opened the front door with his key. He entered with Mary close behind continuing to talk animatedly while obviously enjoying each others company and oblivious to everything else going on around them.

Elizabeth Dickens and Mrs. Hogarth both came down the stairs carrying dishes of water and Dr. Francis Beard followed after them. He came over. 'The child is on its way, it's a waiting game now. I'll return this evening.'

"A day and night of watching and anxiety" followed and Dr.Beard was again in the Dickens household attending Catherine.

After the birth he sought Charles out in his study to

pronounce. 'You've a son Charles and they're both fine. It's a small matter but Catherine can't feed the child so I will send a wet nurse along to you.'

'Francis we're in your debt. I'll go up to her.' Charles escorted Beard to the front door and held it open for him.

He climbed the stairs to the master bedroom where a tearful Catherine sat nursing her baby. 'We have a son.'

'I know Beard told me.' Charles pulled back the cover from the babies face. 'He looks very small.'

'I can't feed him. He's going to love others more than me.'

'Catherine, it's not your fault that you cannot nurse him. He's so small he won't remember who gave him his first sustenance, in truth I cannot remember who gave me mine. He'll be alright, you'll see. Mary will help you and keep you company and I can do my slips. You mustn't be "coss" if I work. Oliver Twist will not write itself.'

'Can we not be on our own?'

'I don't think so. You need help.' He kissed her brow and left her. Catherine wound a ringlet of hair around her finger nervously.

Mary stayed on tutoring the children and working as housekeeper at times, dusting and handing Charles items which he meticulously arranged. Together they continued to inspect properties looking for a larger home away from Furnival Inn's dark box like rooms.

Doughty Street was found, a four floored terraced house with a small back garden. Having a wine cellar, wash house and study, meant for Charles, that it was another achievement. In time he added his own chosen pieces, a grandfather clock, mirrors and a Spanish mahogany sideboard.

One morning Catherine brought a note to Charles while he worked with Mary. 'This has just come for you.'

Charles took it from Catherine and opened it. 'My membership for the Garrick Club is approved.'

'The Garrick Club!' Mary could not hide the admiration in her voice.

Catherine added. 'That's nice dear.'

'Yes, I'm satisfied.' He went back to painstakingly arranging each object.

Mary handed him his paper knife. 'I think this will be best in this position Charles and your small vase also.'

'I do agree my dear.'

Catherine stifled her feelings of irritation as she withdrew. She must try and remember Charles was a creature of ritual and Mary fawned over him. This meant she herself was needed very little and she felt left out; thinking that apart from giving birth she was there only to see that Charles's inspections of the rooms every morning were to his satisfaction and that everything was in its allotted place. The house had to revolve around Charles.

Each day it was his habit to luxuriate in Doughty Street's tiny washhouse/bathhouse. He would sit in a hipbath of cold water bathing and singing noisily, "Let us go and take a walk" enjoying every minute of his new found indulgence while Catherine for the most part involved herself in mundane chores.

Anne Brown, their servant stood in front of her. 'You wanted me Madam?'

'Yes Anne. The master will be bathing every day. He

will bathe in cold water.'

'Cold water Mistress?'

'Yes Anne, cold water.'

A visitor to arrive that morning was Samuel Lawrence who Charles had commissioned to do a portrait of him. He carried an easel, with chalks, crayons and other essentials. Thankfully he put these down and extended his hand. 'My dear Catherine, you know why I'm here?'

'Of course, Charles should be with us at any moment. Please make yourself comfortable. Do you wish to be near the light?'

'That would be advantageous.'

'Please arrange everything as you wish.'

The artist moved a plum covered armchair in hide and erected his easel near the window. As he did so Charles entered wearing a satin waistcoat and while patting his hair checked his appearance in a mirror. He eyed up the moved furniture. 'My dear Lawrence I trust I've not inconvenienced you.'

'I've just arrived.'

'I'll leave you.' Catherine smiled at the artist and left them alone.

'Try this position Charles.' The artist held the back of the chair for Charles to sit in and Charles took the proffered seat.

Checking on how his clothing lay he asked. 'Is this correct?'

'An excellent pose, are you comfortable? It'll take some little time.'

'Yes, I'm at ease.'

'Good.' Samuel began to draw.

'Do you think the new medium of photography will impinge on your work?'

'It may do but for the moment it's not here and long may it be so from my point of view.'

'For now the Artist and Writer have come together.'

'For posterity?' Lawrence worked on.

Charles sat quietly and as still as possible, congratulating himself that at last he was spending money and was able to pay his way and open an account with one of the private banks, Coutts and Company with £500.00 of his hard earned cash. He had assessed the institution to be solid as they had survived when many of the others had failed and he was not looking to deposit his money in a venture which would collapse. He had become friends with the heiress of the banking fortune, Angela Burdett Coutts, rather a plain soul to look at but with a generous heart. She took an interest in those who Charles and his family had been part of, the under class. Together they were seeking to relieve some of the poverty strangling the city. Sitting for the artist he despaired, Catherine didn't like him spending time with Angela. He would placate her! He would take her and Mary out for the evening! They could go and see "Is she his wife"?

With this in mind he took Catherine and Mary to the theatre, returning in their evening clothes they entered the house. The nurse came out of the kitchen. 'Is everything alright?' Catherine asked her.

'Yes Madam.' She slipped back into the scullery to make her cocoa.

Mary yawned. 'I'll go up. I'm so tired.'

'We'll follow you, after we've looked in on Charley.' Charles responded.

As Mary climbed the stairs Catherine asked Charles. 'Do you want a nightcap?'

'I think not, it's late.'

They were on their way to bed when a thud came from somewhere near the landing. They ran to where the noise seemed to come from, Mary's bedroom, to find her lying on the floor. Together they got her onto the bed. Catherine stayed calm but Charles was grief stricken. Almost immediately the nurse appeared, having heard the noise.

'Go and get a doctor.' Charles ordered. She ran down the stairs and out of the front door.

Catherine cried out. 'I must tell Mama.'

'I'll go for her.' Charles hurried away.

Catherine took Mary's shoes off, then her dress and covered her with the coverlet. She sat with her for what seemed an eternity until Charles led a hysterical Mrs. Hogarth into the room. Soon after the nurse brought a doctor back and after examining Mary he gently said. 'I can't do anything for her.'

All present were stunned and it was Catherine who instructed the nurse. 'Take Mama downstairs.'

The nurse manhandled Mrs. Hogarth from the room with Catherine directing her. 'Keep Mama away from here.'

The bedroom went quiet after Mrs. Hogarth's sobbing and the doctor spoke almost to himself. 'We can only keep watch over her.'

Charles seemed to be unaware of anything or anyone save Mary who appeared to stir. He put his arm around her shoulders and she whispered. '"Charles, so kind".' then closed her eyes.

Charles appealed to the practitioner who had been brought. 'What's the matter with her?'

'It seems it's her heart.'

'She's seventeen.'

'Age doesn't always come into it.'

'Can't you do something?'

He tried to take Mary's pulse and shook his head. 'She's gone.'

'She can't have died. She must have fallen into unconsciousness. She'll stir in the next few hours. Haven't you seen such a situation before?'

'Never, she's not unconscious, she has no pulse.'

'I must go and tell Mama.' An emotional Catherine brought her mother back into the room, soothing her. 'We must be brave Mama. It's what she would want of us.'

An insensible Mrs Hogarth kissed Mary and wept over her. A tight lipped Charles got up and looked out of the window. 'I'll arrange the burial.'

The following day Catherine and her mother sat together by Mary's bed when Charles came home after being out. 'Everything's arranged. The undertaker will be along presently.' He stared out of the window with his back to them. 'She was so "young, beautiful and good. Thank God she died in my arms and the last words she whispered were of me".' He turned around and faced Mrs. Hogarth. 'May I take Mary's ring and wear it as my own now?'

Mrs.Hogarth glanced at Catherine, who said nothing. Charles's mother-in-law nodded.

'And I should like a lock of her hair. I shall keep it in a special place.' He came over to the bed and reverently removed the ring from the dead girl's finger to place it on his own.

Mrs. Hogarth fixed her gaze on Catherine but again she did not reply. Mrs. Hogarth's answer was stilted. 'So be it.'

Charles cut a ringlet of Mary's hair to place it in his handkerchief.

'Her clothes, we have an abundance of room, may we keep them here?'

A wearisome look passed between Catherine and her mother. Mrs. Hogarth nodded to Charles.

'One final thing, I will pay for the funeral and I should like to be buried with her.'

Catherine and Mrs. Hogarth eyes met but a word wasn't said.

It was a time of despondency for Catherine and her parents, made very much worse because they couldn't understand the way Charles dealt with the death. He sat in his study looking into space. Anne, especially a solicitous servant to Charles, peeped around the door. 'Dinner is served Sir.'

'I won't be availing myself.'

'There are oysters.'

'No thank you.'

'Very well Sir.' She drew back to meet Catherine on the landing.

'Is the master working Anne?'

'No Ma'am, just sitting.'

Catherine dined alone and after she had finished supper went to the library to find Charles. She attempted to make conversation. 'Did you get any writing done today?'

'I cannot, Oliver Twist isn't writing itself. I just can't work and I can't sleep either. I dream of sweet Mary each night.'

A dismayed Catherine got up and left the room.

Charles's depression did not lift. It was Catherine's birthday and he and she breakfasted together. He sighed. 'Today will not be the same without sweet Mary.'

'It's my birthday and I'm here.'

Charles got up and went around to where Catherine sat. He gave her a small parcel, the size of a piece of jewellery. 'So you are. Here is a memento of the day my dear.' He sat down and it was obvious his mind was not on her birthday.

'Thank you Charles.'

'Yes we will miss sweet Mary.'

Catherine said nothing and the box stayed unopened.

Charles remained somewhat detached, before voicing his thoughts, 'While on the subject of birthdays I've arranged with Forster to celebrate at an inn when our wedding anniversary comes around. It will be on the same day as his birthday.'

Catherine said nothing.

When they went to bed that evening Charles dropped off to sleep but then sat bolt upright. 'Sweet Mary, is it you?' He looked around and when convinced she wasn't with him fell back on his pillows whispering, 'I love you,' stirring as he did so.

Catherine's tears wet the pillow. Resentment tinged her voice, 'she was my sister and you grieve so.'

Waking completely, he realised she had heard his

sentiments and tried to explain, 'I loved her too.'

'Obsessively so.'

'I can't expect you to know how I feel. It's a private matter.'

She turned her back on him.

She wasn't alone in trying to understand Charles. His friends and associates were astounded at the way he conducted himself and his life.

In Ye Olde Cheshire Cheese John Forster sat reading a newspaper and Francis Beard came through the door.

'May I?' Beard indicated an empty chair next to Forster.

'Be my guest.'

Francis seated himself. 'Actually I'm pleased to find you here. I've just heard such nonsense from Walter Landor. He says he's had a letter from Dickens and doesn't know what to make of it. He asked me, "What on earth does it mean"? Dickens says he's fallen in love with Queen Victoria and that he wants to run away to an uninhabited island with a lady. He also asked Landor to burn his letter.'

'I've had such a letter.' John Forster brought out a paper from his pocket and handed it to Francis Beard who sat and read it incredulously.

'Rumours are abroad that Dickens is mad and not for the first time. He seems to have no care to what he says.'

'It's his humour that makes him write that way.'

Charles was attracting a lot of attention and it wasn't all flattering. At home in his study he sat reading a broadsheet and angrily crumpled it, throwing it into the waste paper basket. In the drawing room Catherine was visibly shaking and curled her hair around her finger. She sat with her mother who cautiously spoke. 'Is everything alright?'

'Charles worries me.'

'In what way?'

'He dreams of Mary every night and cries out for her.'

'You have a right to be upset. I thought his grief unseemly, it disturbed me. Have you spoken to him about it?'

'I hardly dare, he will brook no discussion. I've found he has a cruel temper.' She sighed. 'He's always absent somewhere and if he's here he's writing. We've never been on our own since our honeymoon.'

'It's not good enough. The man is clearly at his wit's end. I notice he's using writing paper with black edging. I've had a letter from him thanking me for allowing him to keep Mary's things.'

She took it from her purse and passed it to Catherine, who read "I have never had her ring off my finger by day or night, except for an instant at a time, to wash my hands, since she died. I have never had her sweetness and excellence absent from my mind so long…"

Mrs. Hogarth put her arm around Catherine's shoulder. 'Perhaps when he is more established he'll be less fraught. Your father is committed to do all he can to further Charles's career.'

Catherine sighed. 'I know mother.'

It was pre-arranged that George Hogarth call to take his wife home and he did so at the arranged time. He and his wife had gauged that it might be an opportune moment for George to speak with their son-in-law. He knocked on Charles's shut study door, calling, 'Charles.'

The door was opened.

'Can we discuss a matter, man to man?'

'Assuredly.'

'It's rather delicate but Mrs.Hogarth feels Catherine isn't altogether happy about the sorrow you feel over Mary's death. It's probably nothing but I thought I should mention it. Women are strange creatures but Catherine seems to be taking your grief to heart, so have a care.'

Charles backed into the room, allowing his father-in-law to follow. 'I hardly know what to say. It's never been my intention to hurt. I'll make a point of not distressing her in any way.'

'Good man.' They shook hands and George Hogarth joined his wife and daughter.

But Charles's mood was not the same later in the evening when he went to the master bedroom to find Catherine in bed. He allowed himself to sit down heavily on the edge. 'Are you awake?'

'Yes.'

'Your father tells me you've been spreading lies about my grief for Mary. I won't have it. If I hear more on the matter you will have to go to your parents and retract everything you've said. I expect loyalty under my own roof.' He stood up and went to another room before she could say anything.

They slept apart with their own anguished thoughts.

Breakfast next morning never happened. It remained set and untouched on the dining room table. On getting up Catherine went along the passage and seeing the door of Mary's room ajar she put her head around to see Charles going through her wardrobe. He was bringing each dress out and running his hands over them as they lay on the bed.

Catherine disturbed him. 'I thought I should find you here.'

'It is **my** house.' His manner was icy.

'I understand that Charles. But I must talk to you sometimes. I've got to tell you because it concerns you. I'm having another child.'

He gave her a disbelieving look. 'Again?'

'It seems the time would never be right to tell you.' Catherine left before the tears which she now knew would come, ran down her face.

That night Charles went out alone as was his custom. He did one of his usual walks to Kensal Green cemetery to stand in front of Mary's grave and use his hand to clean the words he had had written on her headstone. "Mary Hogarth 1820 – 1837. Young, beautiful and good. God in his mercy numbered her among the angels at the early age of seventeen".

He called in Ye Olde Cheshire Cheese on the way back home and met an old newspaper colleague. He confided, 'Wild ideas are upon me of going abroad somewhere and writing. I need a change.' They sat drinking for a time and when he unsteadily got home "dead drunk" he entered the bedroom to sit on the side of the bed and fall back on the pillows. Catherine got up and removed his shoes and tie. She lay down at his side to hear him moan. 'Sweet Mary.'

Would he ever let Mary's spirit go? And would he ever come back to her? They had one son and had been married a very short time. There was only a flimsy chance of their marriage succeeding, how much effort did he put into it? Work, the need for money and most of all – a dead sister stood in the way.

# Chapter Five

To Catherine's chagrin Charles continued to follow his own social round largely without her. He made arrangements to dine with Angela Coutts. Besides the fact that he was already depositing his money in her bank, they had a great deal to say to one another as they both worked to alleviate some of the poverty and suffering surrounding them.

Catherine said nothing of his absence at the dinner table but sensed Charles had elected her to remain in the background and like the children of the day "to be seen and not heard".

Another interest Charles followed was "mesmerism". He made numerous visits to attend hypnotic sessions, since meeting the physician involved in controversial events held at University College Hospital. Dr. Elliotson had been the first doctor to use a stethoscope and his methods were thought by some to be questionable. Attending a session one evening Charles noted the assembly's evening clothes while the host carried out the experiment on his assistant, Miss Webb. He sat in the front row as usual.

Remembering this would be his fourth attendance, Charles listened as Doctor John Elliotson began. 'It's gratifying to see you my friends together this evening. As you know I hold the view that the powers of the human body can be controlled by an invisible fluid and through management of this, a sick human can be revived or cured. I'll demonstrate.' He turned to his assistant. 'Miss Webb is our subject and I will show that it is possible to mesmerize her.' He began to make movements with his hands around the woman's head. 'Keep your eyes on me Miss Webb.' He brushed her eyebrows with his thumbs. Her eyes flickered and she was in a trance. John Elliotson stood back. 'She's a perfect subject. If anyone wishes to discuss the method I will do so when I've recalled Miss Webb.' He put his face near to hers and breathed on her. She opened her eyes. 'There we have it, a successful outcome.' He stood back. 'I trust you are well Miss Webb?'

'Yes I am so.'

Her hypnotiser bowed and the audience applauded. Charles was one of the first to approach John Elliotson. 'Let me introduce myself. I'm Charles Dickens.'

'I recognised you Sir.'

They shook hands.

'You have an impressive technique. I would be interested in learning more.'

'Certainly: my dear Sir. If you give your address to Miss Webb I'll be in touch.'

Charles's circle grew as he settled into London's 'science' and literary scene. His affairs scarcely stalled apart from resigning from the Garrick Club because as he told Catherine and Mary, "it was not to his taste".

For Catherine the following months proved to be unsettling. In March 1838 a baby girl was born. She plunged deeper into depression. Having children didn't bring her any closer to Charles; in fact it seemed to lead to more estrangement.

Soon after, following a restless night with the new baby, it resulted in her sleeping late one morning. When she made her way to the room where Charles wrote he did not immediately look up. After seconds he spoke. 'Have you forgotten? No interruptions.' Catherine turned to leave. 'Don't be in a pet. I have something to say. I think the name Mary (Mamie) right for our daughter. Do you agree?'

'After my sister?'

'Yes, of course, after Mary.'

Catherine nodded her head slightly.

'And I have also asked Elliotson to come here so that we may explore his hypnotism theory. I trust you will join in?'

'Yes'. She was learning that she had less to say in her married life than she'd had as one of four sisters under her parent's roof.

'You'll have heard Elliotson has left his post.'

'Yes, I did hear of it.'

'He has enemies but we've agreed that he comes here.'

It was always Charles's intention to use Catherine as his subject and thus he arranged the venue to be his home. The three sat together around a table, Elliotson conducting the meeting. He addressed Charles, 'you observed how I induced a trance like state with Miss Webb, well it's perfectly safe for you to do so with your dear wife.' John Elliotson turned to Catherine. 'You're willing?'

'Yes.' Catherine realised she had very little option but to go along with the wishes of Charles.

John Elliotson began demonstrating with his hands in the air and began directing. 'The patient watches the eyes. As I demonstrated earlier the hands are moved over the patient's head to induce a magnetic sleep. The eyebrows are brushed with the thumbs.' He stroked his own eyebrows. 'And to wake the subject their face is breathed on. Perfectly simple, and now

Mr. Dickens you may mesmerize Catherine.'

Charles stood in front of the seated Catherine, "keep your eyes on me", he instructed. Catherine obeyed and Charles moved his hands around her head brushing her eyebrows with his thumbs as her eyes fluttered and closed. Charles shook his head in amazement. 'I didn't believe it would be so simple.'

'You have power, it's obvious.'

Both men considered their work then John Elliotson spoke, 'she should be returned to us.'

'Yes of course.' Charles breathed on Catherine's face and she opened her eyes.

'Have I slept?'

'You have dear lady.' Elliotson was jubilant.

'A fitting outcome' vouched Charles as he straightened his tie. He'd never doubted that he could control Catherine in this way. His excursion into the 'science' had been entirely fitting.

But hypnotism was not the only matter on Charles's mind and now he would realise another longstanding wish, to see a hanging. To this end, he went with friends Maclise and Henry Burnett to form part of a large crowd hoping to get a sight of the execution outside Newgate prison. A scaffold had been set up and the houses with windows overlooking this had onlookers hanging out. The three went from house to house searching for a window to rent and Charles disclosed what he was thinking. '"Just once I should like to watch a scene like this and see the end of the drama".' He shook his head, 'apparently Courvoisier is somewhat of a scribe.' He recited;
'"You Christians all of every nation,
A warning take by my sad fate –

For the dreadful crimes that I've committed,
I, alas! Repent too late".'

His friends greeted the rhyme with silence and a look of distaste crossed Henry Burnett's face, 'he probably didn't write it at all. They put anything on the broadsheets.'

'Quite true, quite true' Charles agreed. They turned a corner to come to a hovel. The old woman Charles knew stood at the door. He put his hand in his pocket. 'How much would you charge for a room with a view from a window?'

'Ten shillings, Sir: but don't I know you?'

'Not to my knowledge Madam.'

Maclise stepped forward and pushed a note into the old crone's hand. She pointed up the stairs and searched Charles's face with her eyes as they began to climb the rickety steps to the unsavoury upper chamber. In the upstairs room they positioned themselves at the cockroach infested window as the clock struck eight. Before very long Charles spied another writing associate he knew being pushed and shoved backwards and forwards in the crowd. He wondered could Thackeray be attending in order to get material for his manuscripts.

Two hangmen hauled the tottering murderer onto the scaffold. An appointed official snarled "hats off in front!"

Some of the crowd removed their hats, others roared as the felon lifted up his fettered hands to pray. The man was strung up and his body convulsed in its death throes before being cut down and dragged onto a wooden bier. His lifeless corpse was trundled back into the prison after being prodded and spat on throughout its journey. The crowd went on drinking and picking pockets. Prostitutes plied their trade as a woman haltingly followed a little ebony skinned Arab clutching a turnip to his too big, filthy jacket. Screeching the word '"nigger"' she dogged his steps relentlessly down the street and out of sight.

The hanging was a forbidding scene to spend time in yet Charles had never been so at ease with the world. He was no longer one of the unfortunates. He had his own place in society. He had friends and associates, his social circle whirled and days later he invited John Forster to dinner. He confided in his friend, 'I cannot "turn the corner" with any of my writing. Since sweet Mary died I've been unable to write, so there're no slips for you to look at old chap.'

'It's of no consequence, you'll "get up steam" again but there's something delicate I've been waiting to discuss with you Charles. You know about the cheques your father forged, well he's also been trying to borrow from Chapman and Hall.' He lowered his voice. 'I thought I should acquaint you of how the matter stood.'

'The devil he has – he'll be the death of me but I'll settle him one way or another. I'll send him out of London where he can do less harm. That's what I will do.'

'It's an unfortunate business.'

Charles got up and paced the room. 'I'll see him tomorrow.'

There was no delay. He stood on his parent's front doorstep next day. His knock on the door brought his father and he was ushered into the house, 'what brings you here my boy?'

'Can't you guess?'

His father looked uncomfortable.

'It's this business with Chapman and Hall. You've

besmirched my good name for the last time. I've arranged a cottage for you in Devon and you and Mama can go there and keep your fingers out of my business. I'll give you enough to live on and that's more than you deserve.' He stormed out to go further.

He instructed his solicitor to insert in newspapers a notice which made it obvious who he was alluding to. "Certain persons having or purporting to have the same surname of our said client have put into circulation, with a view of more readily obtaining credit thereon, certain acceptances made payable at his private residence or at the offices of his business agents". It concluded that in the future no debts would be paid unless by himself or wife. His relationship with his father was not changing. Debt and all it encompassed was his parent's way of life and they had never considered the consequences.

Relationships of any kind were proving to be difficult, Catherine wanted to keep him on a leash and in his irritation he wrote Maclise asking him to come away. "There are conveniences of all kinds at Margate (do you take me?) And I know where they live". Then Forster and he had a disagreement in his own house over dinner, resulting in personal retorts on both sides. Charles ordered Forster to leave and only a great deal of smoothing over of the situation led to Forster staying after Charles admitted "that he had spoken in passion and would not have said what he said could he have reflected", but it was too much for Catherine, she left the room in tears. It was an unfortunate occurrence as Charles was relying on John more and more to read his proofs and advise on other literary matters.

By now Catherine had given birth to another girl, Kate

(Katey). This third birth did not improve her general health and attempts by Charles to continually pay their way as they considered moving to a handsome house in Devonshire Terrace, surrounded by a large, brick walled garden.

Within months Catherine discovered she was pregnant once more and in the following February Walter arrived. She was again confined to bed and asked Charles to bring her some books to read. In a letter to Forster, he requested "….If you have any literary rubbish on hand, please to shoot it here".

When she recovered enough to leave her bed she sat writing for hours while Charles dictated letters and manuscripts to her and walked about the room frowning. 'That's the last of the letters but I should say I've instructed my solicitor to tell my father to leave England and to go on the continent to live. I don't want him in my sight after he's been obtaining money dishonestly. I won't speak to him and as you know I've placed notices in the leading papers disassociating myself from any responsibility for his debts.'

'Charles, it's hard on them.'

'It may be, but it's time my father acted responsibly.' He combed back a curl of hair. 'Forster and I are out together on an errand in the morning. I shan't be here for lunch.' He paused. 'I meant to tell you I have refused to stand for Parliament.'

'How gratifying that you've been approached a second time but you must do what you consider correct Charles.'

'I do.'

Catherine saw she was extraneous and left to go into the garden where her father had just arrived.

He took hold of her arm. 'I told Anne I would find my

own way in. It's Grandmamma dear, she's died.'

'Poor Grandmamma: We knew it had to come but we'll miss her. She was a fine lady.'

'We will my dear but it brings me to something else which I'm afraid will have to be settled sooner rather than later. Can she be buried in Mary's grave?'

'You understand how Charles is about Mary's grave father?'

'I do and have lived to regret that he ever made the funeral arrangements.'

'Of course I shall ask but I don't know the outcome.'

'Of course my dear, Dickens is an "odd" man and one would not expect an ordinary response. I'll take my leave of you, I'm sorry to give you this task.' George Hogarth left.

Catherine waited until later in the day when she thought Charles would be in a good mood. He sat reading and she went to him to reluctantly open the subject. 'Father came this afternoon to tell us Grandmamma has died. They wish to know if she can be buried in Mary's grave.'

"It would be a trial to me to give up Mary's grave, greater than I can possibly express…The desire to be buried next to her is as strong upon me now as it ever was… I cannot bear the thought of being excluded from her dust".'

Catherine hesitated. 'What shall I say?'

'I suppose I must concede.'

'I shall send one of the servants with a note to Mama and Papa.'

There was a whimpering from the nursery and they both looked up. Footsteps sounded, and Anne's voice talking to Mary.

Charles queried Catherine. 'Do we have sufficient help to look after the responsibilities?'

'I believe so but we'll have to think of tutoring.'

'I wondered if Georgina would care to come and live in, to help in whatever respect she can. She is fifteen and very like Mary. So much of Mary's "spirit shines out in this sister," Should we ask her?'

'If you wish Charles, I prefer to be on my own but you know my feelings.'

'I think it would be advantageous to you to have help and I must escape from this toil. I need to travel. I think America would be a good destination. We could see if it would suit us as a permanent home. It would do us all good, it would widen our horizons.'

'Must we Charles? What about Walter.'

'We can leave him with your mother.'

'I would rather not.' She began to cry.

'"You do cry dismally".' 'It would be cheaper living abroad. We could lease the house out.' He endeavoured to bring her around to his way of thinking. 'My commitments are great, we are a large household.'

Charles's ideas were followed through and the children were left in the care of Fred, family and friends when he and Catherine embarked to go to America.

But before they departed there was a Hogarth family death to come to terms with. George, Catherine's twenty year old brother had to be lowered into his grave.

Sailing the Atlantic, the SS. Britannia battled through mountainous seas and they suffered a great deal from sea sickness on the way over. Their journey was not comfortable, partly because Charles found the stateroom "too little".

On American soil Charles was feted. There were many dinners to attend and for him, visits made to prisons, asylums and institutions, in addition to his writing. He spoke on international copyright, a subject he very much wanted to further and as always kept up a correspondence with John Forster complaining of Catherine. "She falls into and out of every coach or boat". The Americans thought Catherine a lady. Charles at times, attracted a more restrained approval.

Whilst they were away John Dickens did what he was known for, he borrowed and tried to borrow money. Writing to Angela Coutts and the bank of her name he asked for an advance of twenty-five pounds so that he could move back into the city he had been exiled from by his son. He also felt compelled to sell off a little of Charles's work in order to get his hands on ready cash.

On Charles's return to England in a shaggy greatcoat of bear and buffalo skin he made the conscious decision that he would not live in America. He had more than one reason. The fact that his work and that of his contemporaries was being used there without any payment to the authors left a sour taste in his mouth. He knew copyright would be an issue in the future. He disapproved of slavery and could not bear the American habit of spitting in spittoons! He toyed with the idea of using the Americans he had met on tour as characters for his pen but was dissuaded from the idea. Instead he completed American Notes, at times reading them through in the rocking chair he had brought home from the States.

For Catherine, she would remember the period as being very, very unhappy. She tried not to think of the American visit, for while standing looking at Niagara Falls Charles had betrayed his feelings, "...what would I give if the dear girl whose ashes lie at Kensal Green had lived to come so far along with us..." He even seemed to avoid her in bed, and she knew it wasn't imagination. It was 1844 when she next had his child.

She lay in bed and he stood looking down at her and the new baby. 'We are growing in numbers. So many responsibilities! I think "Responsibilities" a good name for them.' He sat down on the side of the bed.

'That's how you see us, "Responsibilities," you prefer your pleasures rather than us.'

'Nonsense.'

'Are you not going to look at him?'

'"I decline on principle, to look".' 'I must write some letters.'

He walked out of the room and Catherine began winding her hair on her finger. Why was he like this? How long could she endure his coldness?

In his study Charles drew pen and paper to him. He began to write and then read out. 'I declined "on principle to look at the latter object".'

Next day as he strolled down the London streets with a friend he told him. 'I am restless, I cannot settle to work here. I intend looking at the viability of finding a home in Europe. Georgina may come with us.'

'Will that work?'

'It will, if I make it.'

'Is Catherine recovering?'

'She would be if she would let herself. For myself I am not clear that I particularly wanted another son. I want an escape. I am dead sick of the Scottish tongue in all its moods and tenses.'

'Georgina is Scotch.'

'That's different.'

'I could spend some time abroad.'

'I knew I could count on you. We will arrange it as soon as I return. We will have a trip together but now regrettably I must go home.'

'Should we call in The Grapes before you do?'

'So be it.'

'Do you know The Grapes are calling themselves The Surrey Music Hall?'

'I'd heard.'

Time was spent in the inn and Charles as usual observed his fellow man, always seeking new material to characterise.

Before long with a friend he undertook more of the work Angela was offering to finance. Field Lane Ragged School was situated in Saffron Hill. The "school" was as "little" as he remembered Warren's Blacking Factory, almost leaning crazily and seeming as though it could not remain standing much longer. The years had left their mark of decay on the building and the children appeared to be suffering from a type of mange, destitute and without hope. As a notable he was able to make his mark and help those who were unable to help themselves.

# Chapter Six

Charles made his own plans and taking the children, Catherine and Georgina with him, set out for Dover. They sailed by ship to Genoa. After moving from their first leased residence they rented the largest palatial home to be found in the area, Palazzo Peschiere. Nestling in its own gardens, with terraces and fountains, it commanded a beautiful view over Genoa. Yet in such a setting his restless spirit again disturbed him. There was an evening when he sat up in bed murmuring, 'Dear Mary, "give me some token you have really visited me"!' His words roused Catherine and he told her of the dream.

He couldn't know how much pain she felt at his attitude regarding her dead sister, but did he? Mary still haunted his memory, Catherine died a little more inside.

Writing Forster of the encounter he told him "....I recognised the voice....I knew it was poor Mary's spirit. I was not at all afraid, but in great delight, so that I wept very much and stretching out my arms to it called it, 'Dear'...."

Charles's manner affected Catherine. She was no trapeze artist, yet she walked a tight rope. She could be accused of any transgression at any moment by Charles and have no defence. She strove to please him but she grew ever more nervous. When at home her involvement with the children was extensive and although there was 'help' to do laundering, shopping, entertaining, etc. for such a large household, each day was very full yet in her quiet moments she compiled a cookery book, "What shall we have for dinner". Its menus were rather lavish and could not be widely adopted but she made every effort to make her mark. She had not given up completely – yet.

In time Charles finished the manuscript he was writing, The Chimes and he purposely made his way back to London alone to launch it.

This done he returned to Catherine who had been "disconsolate" at being left behind once again. He hoped to lift her out of one of her black moods and so he asked her out on one of his walks. They turned out of their rented house onto the boulevard and encountered a couple linking arms. Charles was instantly charmed by the attractive Swiss lady. The gentleman would have passed by but Charles lifted his hat and stood blocking the way. 'We are all visitors to this country, I believe.'

'I take it we are.'

'I'm Charles Dickens, author and this is my wife Catherine. I'm afraid I have no cards printed, we've just arrived.'

'Emile de la Rue; Swiss banker. May I present my wife Augusta?'

The two men shook hands and the ladies minutely observed their opposites fashion from their respective countries.

'Would you care to call after dinner this evening?' Charles flicked a leaf from his jacket.

De la Rue turned to his wife. 'My dear?'

'Charming.'

'Should we say eight o'clock then?' Charles queried.

'That will be convenient.'

Emile and Charles raised their hats and walked on.

The day drew to its close and the newly acquainted

four sat chatting around the fire for some time. Emile confided 'unfortunately my wife is tormented by a neurological condition. The doctor refers to it as a nervous "tic".'

'How very unfortunate, but may I be of assistance? I have for some time been interested in animal magnetism and may be able to help your lady.'

De la Rue's face coloured.

Augusta didn't wait for her husband to answer, 'I would be willing Emile.'

De la Rue was obviously suspicious. 'Would this involve hypnotism?'

'It would, but I have practiced the art. Catherine can vouchsafe I've done this with her very easily.'

Catherine reluctantly nodded.

De la Rue acceded 'very well, I consider it will best be done in our own home.'

'That can be arranged, when will we say? Tomorrow 10.30 a.m.'

'Very well, we will see you then.'

Charles spent a great deal of time with his "patient" and Catherine grew eternally tired of the situation declaring, 'you promised to take me to see some of the sights and instead you've been "treating" Augusta every day.'

'Your jealously is intolerable.'

'Yes that's true. I am insecure and you've made me so. From the very first days of our marriage you showed me you could prefer my sisters to me. I never see you, you're occupied incessantly.'

Even his lisp could not hide the hostility in his voice. 'Of course I'm always occupied. The truth is that I am

78

responsible for the family I've left in England as well as a growing number here. You've never gone hungry; I've taken care of that. Your life before we met was not as mine. I had no one to give me counsel and scarce any schooling.'

'You say you had no one to counsel you, but no-one was given more help. You yourself told me your mother secured your first job for you. Your father got you into The Mirror of Parliament and your uncle put a word in for you to join The Morning Chronicle, as well as Papa helping you. That seems a great deal of support.'

'I will not listen to this. I only need to look at another and you sulk. Furthermore the situation is not helped by your no longer speaking to the de la Rues. You know my interest is professional.'

'I don't know that. I need you Charles. Have you forgotten I'm having a child?'

Charles gave her a bleak look. 'No, I've not forgotten and have tried to explain your behaviour to the de la Rues. It's crass that you will not speak to Augusta. Your temper brings on the nervous anxiety you are experiencing. You must apologise to Augusta and Emile.'

'I won't apologise.'

His face darkened "I have assured Emile that no occupation of any sort or kind will change or affect the intensity of my desire to do his wife good". They stood facing each other until he walked out.

Catherine was shaken. She was now standing up to Charles. She didn't have a great deal to lose. She'd already lost his love. She knew he had parodied her in his The Cricket on the Hearth. He had shown her up as Tilly Slowboy the great clumsy nursemaid and that hurt a great deal. She sensed her assumption to be right in believing her husband's thoughts were with other women, even a dead woman. He'd reminded Catherine of his loss. "This day years ago, poor dear Mary died...."

At home his infatuations had not gone by unobserved. One newspaper reported that when watching a piano recital by a Miss Weller, Charles "kept his eyes firmly on her every movement". Charles found the opportunity to write in Ms. Weller's album. "I love her dear name which has won me some fame, but Great Heaven how gladly I'd change it"!

Catherine read the newspaper account and concluded she stood in his way. He didn't care if she understood this.

A friend of Charles, T. J. Thompson, who was also interested in Christiana Weller, received a letter from Charles. Not able to believe what had been written, he again read. "Good God what a madman I should seem, if the incredible feeling I have conceived for the girl could be made plain to anyone"! Dickens was a married man and he knew he himself intended to have her! He had told Charles that much!

Charles's inexplicable ways continued to surface. He requested Christina Weller that she save the dress he first saw her in for him. "Let it be laid up in lavender. Let it never grow old, fade......" He later confessed on first seeing her that he "saw an angel's message in her face that smote me to the heart".

Catherine learnt of his wishes and it added to her sense of loss and bewilderment.

Even so, given their strained relationship the years continued to be eventful. Despite miscarriages, in 1845, Alfred was born, in 1847 Sydney, Henry in 1849 and Dora in 1850.

Charles wasn't without his dilemmas. He thought long and hard over more than one threatened action against him in court. His style of writing was to characterise those around him, family, friends and acquaintances. They were all material for his stories and it brought him trouble. The depictions weren't always kind and one lady dwarf took exception about her "personal deformities".

Yet at the same time he joined others in criticising the Pre-Raphael paintings, he wrote;

"A Criticism of Millais' Christ in the House of His Parents, 1850.

You behold the interior of a carpenter's shop. In the foreground of that carpenter's shop is a hideous, wry-necked, blubbering, red-headed boy, in a bed gown; who appears to have received a poke in the hand, from the stick of another boy with whom he has been playing in an adjacent gutter, and to be holding it up for the contemplation of a kneeling woman, so horrible in her ugliness, that (supposing it were possible for any human creature to exist for a moment with that dislocated throat) she would stand out from the rest of the company as a Monster, in the vilest cabaret in France, or the lowest gin-shop in England...

Wherever it is possible to express ugliness of feature, limb, or attitude, you have it expressed. Such men as the carpenters might be undressed in any hospital where dirty drunkards, in a high state of varicose veins, are received.

Charles Dickens.

Household Words, 15<sup>th</sup> June 1850".

And:

"Letter to the Times, 7<sup>th</sup> May 1851.

We cannot ensure at present as amply or as strongly as we desire to do, that strange disorder of the mind or the eyes which continues to rage with unabated absurdity among a class of juvenile artists who style themselves P.R.B. which being interpreted, means Pre-Raphael brethren. Their faith seems to consist in an absolute contempt for perspective and the known laws of light and shade, an aversion to beauty in every shape, and a singular devotion to the minute accidents of their subjects, including, or rather seeking out, every excess of sharpness and deformity. Mr.Millias, Mr.Hunt, Mr.Collins – and in some degree – Mr.Brown the author of a huge picture of Chaucer, have undertaken to reform the art on these principles. The Council of the Academy, acting in the spirit of toleration and indulgence to young artists, have now allowed these extravagances to disgrace their walls for the last three years, and although we cannot prevent men who are capable of better things from wasting their talents on ugliness and conceit, the public may fairly require that such offensive jests should not continue to be exposed as specimens of the waywardness of these artists who have relapsed into the infancy of their profession.

Charles Dickens".

Personally he remained adamant to his children that "their father's name was their best possession" and as always, his work and acting continued to buoy him up. With Catherine at his side, he met a young actress, Mary Boyle and she captivated him. He flirted with her in Catherine's presence and wrote her affectionate notes at intervals which he considered a "joke".

Catherine did a great deal of thinking, brooding and worrying that made her "exceedingly unwell". The doctors described her condition as a "nervous collapse". She knew when Charles had written a letter to Dr. Wilson asking him to look after her he had described her condition as a "nervous one", of "a peculiar kind". The attention Charles had paid her sisters caused her pain. Why had he married her? His obvious preference was for her siblings. Mary wasn't with them now but Georgina was and she didn't believe Charles was trying to mask the admiration he felt towards Georgina and other women. In fact she could have thought the cruel streak in him made him enjoy her distress. She sensed her parents and other family members shared her feeling of apprehension. They had voiced their disapproval to her of Charles's over friendliness towards Georgina for months now and unease at her accompanying him on his long meanders into the countryside around London.

But there was one walk he did alone. He had to say goodbye to the Marshalsea and that was a very private matter, not to be shared with anyone else, however close. He found it difficult to set out along the path that led him there. He had been meaning to go back to the prison for some years since it last closed its spiked gates on those unfortunates, such as his father, but he had not cared to go its way. Now wandering down Angel Court he looked up at the washing hung out on poles and dusty linnets swinging in rusting birdcages. Further ahead he could see three brass bells swinging, the pawnbrokers! As a child it had been his task to go and take what "little" was left of value from Mrs. Roylance's lodging house or the Marshalsea prison in exchange for a small amount of money until his parents could redeem the item and hopefully retrieve their property. More often than not the goods were never recovered because there was a time limit put on them the day they were taken into the shop. He looked straight ahead; he wouldn't even glance in "uncle's" window. The ambience of London old town had not changed but he was taken aback when he confronted the old prison. It had become something else, changing its form and used for a different purpose. The clanging gates had gone and it had lost its menacing aspect. He knew debtors' prisons were closing down all over London and suddenly he felt a lot safer. If there were no debtors' institutions, he could never be incarcerated in any one of them.

He viewed the desolation of some of the "Rookeries". Demolition had left piles of rubble and little else. Strangely, the fetid smell that had always hung around the area was in fact more accentuated, as though it had been released from the very bricks and mortar. He wondered if the houses left standing would now become even more overcrowded. Every nation under the sun had made their way to the capital and they had not always co-existed easily. Fights and murders were commonplace. It was still a den of iniquity, yet the earth was yielding up a new beginning, New Oxford Street was being born.

Retracing his steps he caught up with a gypsy caravan. It's probably on its way to Leck Fields he thought. From the side and back of the van hung pots, pans and mugs all strung together by the handles, jugs and a miscellany of items. The narrow lane opened out into one of the new squares and as he passed the van he read on its side, **FORTUNES TOLD**. He had seen three miserable children hanging out of the back and the ageing horse with grizzled thin hair was led by a disreputable looking individual. The man was past his prime and Charles wondered who the children belonged to. Years ago he could have disappeared off the face of the earth and his parents would not have known until he failed to turn up on one of his visits to them.

Arriving home he had many distractions, Fred was trading on his name to obtain credit and now their father lay very ill. He hailed a cab to arrive at Keppel Street. He hurried into the small house and found his mother sitting at his father's bedside. 'How is he?'

'He hasn't moved or spoken all day. He doesn't know me.'

'Courage Madam, he has undergone a dreadful ordeal. He may rally yet.' Charles took hold of his father's hand.

They sat together for what seemed to both of them to be an eternity.

Elizabeth Dickens pushed the grey hair back from her husband's brow. '"D" my "D".' She sobbed over her dying husband.

Charles scrutinized his father's face and let his hand drop from his own. 'He's gone mother.' For a time they sat together in silence. 'I'll pay all father's bills, don't worry on that score and I'll see to it that you don't want.' It was the end of a chapter. Charles considered the many calls from his purse as he took his leave knowing he was soon to buy the eighteen roomed Tavistock House set in a large garden near Tavistock Square. The new very expensive home lay in a very prestigious district in the city.

Catherine and Charles could not help but see the marriage was becoming more strained and bordering on a breakdown. They were both trying to keep up appearances as Catherine was again confined in bed. She looked nervously at Charles as he entered their bedroom. He gave the newest arrival, Edward, a brief look. 'A boy?'

'Yes'.

'We resemble a lying- in-hospital and all the children belong to us.'

Catherine couldn't answer.

'You are dismal. You must try and rally yourself. We all have difficulties. Rest while I work. I must prepare for my reading tour.' He went to his study and began writing, reading out the words as he wrote. 'Catherine has had her baby. I'm not quite clear that I wanted the latter.' Putting his note into an envelope he drew another sheet of paper to him and wrote a fellow lady novelist, that he thought of "interceding with the Bishop of London to have a little service in St. Paul's beseeching that I may be considered to have done enough towards my countries population". He ended his letter writing to Forster explaining, 'the presence of my wife aggravates me.'

He then absented himself once more to further some of the work he was engaged in with Angela Burdett Coutts. She wished to find a good spot to build housing for the very poor but it would have been unsafe if she had taken a step into the maze of back alleys to look around. Where he stood, Flower and Dean Street had a dire reputation. The police patrolled these areas in twos! Miss Coutts had the money to bring any plan to fruition but Charles knew London and he would advise her. Coming to Bermondsey, he found such a place with "wooden houses like horrible old packing cases full of fever for a countless number of years". They looked as if they weren't pulled down they would fall down just as others had previously done with people inside them. Making his way home he expected Catherine would make a scene. She knew Angela wished to marry elsewhere, why couldn't she realise he was not acting improperly? She'd turned sullen and when they spoke, she complained. He was certain she did not or could not understand him. Her own needs were of paramount importance to her and no-one else mattered at all.

At dinner, as expected, she upbraided him. 'I agree it is a good thing to build houses for the poor but you are needed here, I never see you.'

'Nonsense, I can't stay locked up in the house for ever.'

'I don't mean you to stay locked up in the house for ever.'

'What do you want then? Are you jealous of Angela too?'

'You know I'm not. She's my friend also but people are talking, they're saying you are well acquainted with the "low life".'

'And where've you heard that? No doubt, your mother's words again.'

'It wasn't mother.'

'You can't expect me to believe that.'

'Well it's true. Doing what Angela wants is taking up any free time you might have ever had. Building the "Home for fallen women" has meant that some people believe you spend too much time with them.'

'Well the women are all on their way to Australia now. You can't be jealous of any of them any more but I expect you'll find something else to complain of, you always do. I'm heartedly tired of all this.'

Charles got up and pushed back his chair, leaving the table. 'Woman you are mad.'

She bit her lip as he slipped further and further away from her.

Next morning Charles set out on another excursion away from home and could not refrain from writing her, to strongly recommend, not insist, that she write Augusta de la Rue a friendly and sympathetic letter...."Your position beside these people is not a good one, is not an amiable one, a generous one - is not worthy of you at all.... You have it in your power to set it right at once by writing her a note to say that you have heard from me, with interest of her sufferings and her cheerfulness.... that if you should ever be thrown together again.... you hope it will be for a friendly association without any shadow upon it". He said he would never enquire whether she had followed his recommendation.

She dutifully wrote the desired letter and sat and cried. She too was changing, she hated the position he put her in. If he couldn't control her, he behaved like a spoilt child. Yet he had never been that! Her resolve to make the marriage work was gone. She guessed the small child at her side would be the last baby she would ever have. Charles didn't even want to be near her now!

He had made it very plain where his priorities lay. He would soon travel abroad on a two month jaunt with his new friend, Wilkie Collins and Augustus Egg. Egg attracted attention because he was slight and had an enormous brow bulging over his spectacles while Collins was a "womaniser" and thought to be "vulgar". Egg seemed also to be taking an interest in Georgina as well as Charles. Catherine knew she would not be expected to make the trip.

Before he took his leave he wandered the country lanes with "Georgie". 'It's so peaceful out here. No distractions. No Catherine. No servants. No children.'

'Charles' she remonstrated.

'Just you and I.' His face had a look of pain. 'I wish it could always be so.'

She searched his face.

'You know I want to keep on loving you?'

She nodded.

'May I?'

Her answer was low. 'Yes.'

'I feel trapped. Somehow I have to change my life.'

'Charles, it's my fault. I'm causing you problems.'

'Shush. Don't say that, it's not true.' He began kissing her repeatedly until a feeling of ecstasy and oblivion engulfed them both.

Elsewhere for once it wasn't the Dickens marriage being discussed it was Charles's writing. In their club Thackeray and John Macrone sat reading newspapers. Macrone looked up. 'There are some dreadful reviews on Dickens's work. Bleak House has been called "twaddle".'

'Dickens won't like that. He wouldn't give any review credence if he didn't agree with it. In fact it's hard to see who or what he approves of nowadays. He seems at odds with the world.'

# Chapter Seven

Catherine's sense of foreboding regarding Georgina intensified. She couldn't put her finger on the change that was occurring, yet she wondered. Was it the fact that Georgina now treated her as the inexperienced sister and seemed to regard herself as the wiser adult? She didn't know but it was there. "Aunt Georgie", tutor to the children, appeared indispensable. At times she wrote Charles's letters for him and his pet name for her was "Georgie". He even called her "the Virgin" and that seemed a little too familiar to Catherine. Charles called herself and Georgina "my ladies", obviously "Georgie" was her equal and more? It was unnerving to admit that she had a growing mistrust of her younger sister.

She had confided in her parents and they shared her misgivings. They'd spoken to Georgina on their disapproval and her allegiance to Charles but it had resulted in a heated exchange. She wouldn't listen to her parents. The family wondered if Georgina could be Charles's mistress. The position was indefinable but on Charles's return Georgina had been sent to Bologna. Charles had tasked her with looking at the suitability of renting a larger holiday property. She sighed; Georgina's presence wasn't missed. She didn't need the snide remarks that at times, came from Georgina. She had hoped her own position would be normalised without "Georgie", but it hadn't happened. She was totally inadequate when competing with her sister. She looked down at the tight bodice of her gown; child bearing had not improved her figure and she didn't have Charles's vitality, she couldn't keep up with his boundless energy. Georgina seemed so much more able than she. There could be no contest beside her sister.

On the other hand Georgina looked radiant. Their mother had remarked on it and her putting on a few pounds led them both to think the unthinkable, could she be pregnant with Charles's child? Catherine rejected this grotesque notion, she did not want to believe such a betrayal and she thought she knew Charles enough to understand that risking his reputation would be unthinkable.

Thoughts went around and around in her head. The feeling of being the third person in the marriage wouldn't go away. She remembered when they first met, he was penniless yet he seemed to know what he wanted. Now he considered himself "inimitable".

As time went on she had had much less to say to him and to her sister. They were polite to one another but distant. A stand-off seemed to exist between them. It was strange, all these years she had not admitted, even to herself, that Charles wasn't the man he strove to show the world. For the first time in her life she was hearing his lisp and found it unattractive. She knew he made jokes and ridiculed her to his friends regarding what he considered her clumsiness. Her depression deepened, she realized he didn't want her as a wife and asked herself where would his inclinations take him? It was unlikely that as a couple, they would stay as they were. She was full of trepidation.

Charles had less time for soul searching. His role was to plan ahead and make enough money to cover every eventuality.

It was a miserable time for all whilst Georgina was

away and Charles seemed to be even more remote. The situation was made unbearable by unspeakable whisperings reaching London from India.

Mrs.Hogarth grew very agitated by what she heard while sitting in a coffee house with a friend. She catapulted into Tavistock House when she knew Charles wasn't there and made sure Anne Brown was out of earshot. 'Is she not back yet?' she demanded of Catherine.

'Do you mean Georgina?'

'Yes, I mean Georgina.'

Catherine shook her head, 'no she isn't.'

'Do you know what's happened?'

'No mother.'

'She's the talk of London. She's had a baby and do you know what she's called him? She's called him Charles Bulwer Lytton Dickens. What is she thinking of?'

Was her mother really telling her all this? 'It can't be true mother.'

'It's true, where do you think she's been all this time? She's only supposed to be looking at a holiday house for him, but she's in Calcutta and shall I tell you why? It's because she thinks we'll never find out what she's been up to. That's why she's gone right around the world and besides there are English people in the vicinity.'

Catherine tried to persuade her mother. 'She wouldn't want to mix with the English. She would keep herself to herself.'

'She might not, she's so smitten with the "genius" as she calls him and she's been found out, how else would we have heard about it.'

'I don't know mother. I'm at a loss but I don't think she would name a child so, they are traceable names, names Charles uses in his own family and you know he attaches great importance to them.'

The door knob was turned with difficulty and Edward toddled in. Catherine jumped up and led him away by the hand to Anne Brown.

Returning to her mother they sat together in silence until Catherine picked her words carefully, 'she wouldn't be so unwise as to do such a thing.'

'Wouldn't she? I don't know my own daughter since she met Charles Dickens.'

Catherine spoke softly, 'he probably thinks such a birth could never be proved.'

'I think Charles Dickens could disprove anything. He believes entirely in his own worth.' She paused for breath. 'He's convinced he can write anything off.'

For mother and daughter time passed dismally. There were other rumours circulating the city and time dragged until Catherine and the children joined Charles in Bologna. Georgina was there but there was no child and Charles seemed to keep her at arm's length! Catherine wondered at this. Questions disturbed her, was he now realising on the one hand how naïve Georgina could be or how stubbornly at times she worked to get what she wanted? Perhaps the name that had been given to his child was too revealing? Did he see what a danger the name could pose? And if there were a child, where was it? Was Charles blaming Georgina for the birth in some inexplicable way? As he had seemed to hold her responsible for the number of children they had.

She agonised over the rumour, if it were true, the child would make a difference to all their lives but would Charles attempt to silence his critics in his usual way by publicly printing his innocence? Something was amiss. She felt sick. Had Georgina given the rumoured child such a name because she felt she was leaving him so little of herself and Charles or was it an act of defiance? She had to admit to herself that she didn't know her sister or husband well enough to arrive at any answer.

Over the coming weeks she saw him put a little distance between himself and "Georgie". He now called her Georgina more often and Catherine questioned whether he was behaving more like his written characters in their sexless sister/brother relationships. She could only guess. He was a master at keeping his real feelings hidden and secrets if he chose; were his forte.

When they returned to England, Charles continued with his multiple projects. In his working life he wrote many letters and received a considerable number in return. More and more begging letters were being sent him; at times involving prostitution and he would invariably turn to Angela Coutts.

Together they continued to collaborate in trying to reform the women. His thoughts were wry thinking of when the "ladies of the night" had been sent to Australia to make new lives. The situation had got out of hand and on the way over some of them had reverted to their ancient profession with the crew. He had lost some trust in his own and Miss Coutts's ability to change their long existing practice. There had also been trouble in the home they had been sent from.

Within Tavistock House's walls with all its mysteries,

a miserable, questions unanswered, interval continued for Catherine yet she was uniquely placed to read her husband's every mood. It was remarkable how her instincts didn't play her false. She guessed Charles was looking for distractions elsewhere besides those she knew of but she couldn't know how closely they threatened.  He was leaving with Wilkie Collins later in the day to go to Paris and was tidying his desk prior to his departure. His personal effects were meticulously laid out in front of him. He straightened his paper knife and turned to the day's tray of delivered letters. Recognising handwriting on one of the envelopes he slit it with his knife, smiling as he read, 'Maria.' He remembered how he had said to her years earlier, 'you know I love you' and she had been cool towards him.  Had she changed her mind? He wondered. He read the letter twice and drew a sheet of paper in front of him. He began to write, at the same time speaking aloud. '"I forget nothing of those times".' He continued writing, sealed the letter and put it in his pocket. He re-read his old sweetheart's letter and hid it away in a small drawer in his desk locking it. Walking to the post box he dropped his note in and returned home.

Still dressed in his outdoor clothes he went from room to room inspecting drawers. He stopped in front of a mirror to adjust his gold chain and pin, tighten his enormous tie then went downstairs to the underground kitchen where he found Cook going over a shopping list with Georgina.

Catherine sat at a table writing labels for jams. He spoke curtly to her. 'See to it that the servants keep the drawers in order. It's your responsibility to see that they do their work. Your "indolence" mustn't be copied by them.'

Catherine answered in an almost inaudible voice. 'I do try to be a dutiful wife.'

'A man needs more than that. I will write you from Paris.' He briefly kissed her on the forehead. He turned to his sister-in-law, 'goodbye Georgina.' Collecting his packed suitcases he struggled through the front door, banging it behind him.

A cab, with Wilkie Collins inside waited. Charles joined him and they were driven off. On the way Charles told Collins briefly of the letter he'd just received.

Once ensconced in Paris the first thing Charles did in the hotel bedroom was to swiftly pen a letter. He was interrupted by Wilkie, 'are you writing to Maria?'

'Yes.'

'Is it nearly finished?'

'Yes, then I'm at your disposal for the rest of the day.'

'That's the spirit; shall we go to an art gallery?'

'I should say so.'

'What did Maria say in her letter?'

'She asked me to purchase some jewellery for her and the children.'

'Will you?'

'Yes.' Charles wrote on as Wilkie Collins preened himself in front of a mirror and took a large quantity of opium.

Charles looked up, 'does that help you at all?'

'It deadens the pain I have and tonight I'll take laudanum. It'll send me to sleep.'

'Well I shouldn't take too much if I were you.'

They saw the sights, did some writing and made their way back to London where Charles sent Maria the brooches and velvet collar with a clasp of blue stones he had bought her at her request. Eagerly waiting further news he went through his mail and recognised her writing. He opened her letter, read it with a smile and picked up his pen to write and say the first words, '"My dear Maria".' He swiftly wrote and sealed his letter to post it to an agreed address, other than her home, then hid away the received note in his desk.

That evening in the men only room of Ye Olde Cheshire Cheese he and Wilkie Collins sat having a meal. 'So do tell me all' Wilkie awaited the details regarding Maria.

'She and I have arranged that she'll call at a time when Catherine is "not at home" and I'll receive her.'

'That's a well thought out scheme.'

'I consider it so.'

'You're living dangerously.'

'Do you think so?'

'Yes I do. If word gets out you could be finished as a writer.'

'I don't intend for word to get out and I will refute accusations. Accusations must be proven.'

Wilkie shrugged his shoulders. 'You're learning fast.'

'I am. My marriage is a "total smash".'

Time didn't go quick enough for Charles but eventually the day came when Catherine left the house and climbed into her phaeton to be driven away by the manservant. Charles watched out of the window and then went around the house straightening pictures and furniture. He checked his appearance in front of the mirror then went into his study.

Outside Maria Winter was driven up in a cab. She stepped from it and paid the driver, knocking on the front door to have it opened by the maid. She coyly enquired, 'is your Mistress at home?'

'I'm sorry Ma'am she's not in, but the Master is.'

'Very well, I'll see him.'

The maid stood to one side and Maria entered to be ushered to Charles's study. The maid opened the door and announced, 'Mrs.Winter, Sir.'

Charles sat at his desk and Maria entered. He found himself viewing an expanding, simpering forty four year old matron with two missing teeth. His enthusiasm for the meeting evaporated. He couldn't help himself, his expression changed from pleasurable anticipation to shock. She was no better than Catherine!

*No-one has ever looked like that at me before* Maria thought. She sensed his distain as she came forward and extended a hand. 'Charles,' she wondered what he would say after such a look.

'Mrs.Winter.'

'Call me Maria, you always used to.'

'That was a long time ago.'

'Yes it was but I'm just the same, if a little older.'

'As we all are. Time doesn't stand still I fear. Please be seated and I'll ring for tea.'

Maria sat down and Charles rang the bell chord to call a servant. Anne appeared and he ordered, 'we'll have tea. Please serve it in the drawing room as usual.' When Anne scurried away Charles asked, 'shall we go to the drawing room? It's more comfortable there.'

His guest's eyes travelled the room. 'Is this your study? Where you conceive all your great stories to make their way into the world?'

'You're too kind, but yes, I write here. Shall we go to the drawing room?' He offered Maria his arm, which she took and they departed to have tea.

'If father had not chosen elsewhere for me I might have been mistress of this house.'

'Destiny is a strange affair is it not?'

'It is Charles and it can be so hard.'

Charles led his visitor to the drawing room where she seated herself comfortably. There was a brief pause while Charles uncharacteristically wondered what he should say then Georgina entered. 'Oh I'm sorry. I didn't know you had a visitor.'

Charles hoped his relief was not too evident. 'It's of no account, come and meet Mrs. Winter, a friend of yesteryear.' He turned to Maria. 'Mrs. Winter, may I present Georgina, my wife's sister.'

'I'm pleased to make your acquaintance.' Georgina seated herself.

Charles walked to the door. 'I'll go and get another cup.'

There was a brief silence then Maria asked, 'you live here?'

'Yes, I help. It's a very large household.'

'It must be stimulating for you.'

'Yes, I would say it is. There are many guests.'

'How interesting my dear! Did you know Charles and I were almost betrothed a long time ago?'

'How very extraordinary that is!' She didn't trouble to hide her surprise.

Charles returned with a cup and saucer to have tea poured by Georgina. They sat with only the sound of a ticking clock as they sipped their drink. Georgina put her cup on the table. 'I was looking for Cook so I'll go and find her, if you'll excuse me.'

'Must you?' Charles murmured.

'I believe I should.'

When the door was closed behind Georgina, Maria sighed, 'a pretty girl, almost as I was.'

The remark momentarily threw Charles. 'Yes she's an asset to the household.' He paused, looking for something to say. 'I can send you some theatre tickets if you wish. I myself may even attend the performance.'

'How wonderful that would be.'

Charles sought to engineer the conversation to its close. 'I expect Catherine will be returning soon.'

'Then I must go. Time flies when one spends it agreeably, don't you think? '

'Most certainly: most certainly.'

She stood up and Charles escorted her to the front door. She held out her hand, 'just like old times.'

'Indeed. May I call you a cab?'

'I'll walk, I enjoy it.'

'Very well Mrs. Winter.'

'We must meet again.' She stood expectantly on the step and when Charles didn't answer she walked off along the pavement showing she had a slow gait.

Charles closed the door and leant against it then went to his study and poured himself a large hock.

Often in the course of his walks he called in at

Highgate cemetery. He knew the way to Mary's grave by heart. He dusted the gravestone and stood there. *Can I ever be happy again? Can I ever escape the drawbacks of this present life?* By now he was very aware that Catherine was not the woman of his dreams. He wandered home through the back lanes of London.

Over time he was to find Maria was not finished with him, although he had seen enough of her. She sent her maidservant with a message. 'Mrs. Winter was disappointed not to see you at the theatre.'

Georgina passed the message on to Charles as he sat at his desk. His expression changed. 'I must stop all this nonsense.'

'I agree. "She is fearfully silly and commonplace".'

He picked up his pen, reading as he wrote. '"I am grieved if you suspect me of not wanting to see you but I can't help it; I must go my way, whether or no".'

He was just beginning to think he would hear no more of her when she came to be standing on the step asking. 'Is Mrs. Dickens at home?'

'Yes.' The maid's answer was not what she wanted to hear.

She prevaricated. 'I'll call again another day.'

Charles watched her from an upper window as she moved awkwardly along the street. He dismissed her from his mind and Catherine was unaware that there had been a caller to the house.

Mrs. Hogarth worked on the same principle as Maria Winter only she tried to call when she knew Charles was not at home. On one such a day she arrived to take off her bonnet and collapse into a chair. 'Your father dined at the club yesterday and the latest news is that John Forster has been appointed as the Lunacy Commission Secretary. What does he know about lunacy?' She paused for breath. 'No doubt Charles will be quizzing him on the subject.'

'Mother, I've found John Forster to be a decent man, he often opposes Charles.'

'That's why they keep falling out!'

'Mother, Charles has already been advised against having me committed. I don't think John would agree to go along with Charles's wishes. John has probably been given the post because of his literary achievements. You know that's how are things are done.'

'Who knows what any of them get up to when they're given power? He's Charles's friend.'

The front door banged and Charles's voice could be heard talking to his manservant. Mrs. Hogarth pursed her lips and went quiet for the remainder of her visit. They heard Charles giving orders to his man then the door shut as he left with the manuscript he had forgotten.

Charles had a lot on his mind. He was about to spend time in France, perhaps on his own or in the company of friends, possibly Georgina. The Crimean War had ended and Paris was an enchanting city.

He crossed the channel many times and even putting a stretch of water between himself and his in-laws could not lessen his hostility towards them. Ceasing to make any attempt to hide his feelings towards Catherine's parents he wrote a friend "…. I cannot bear the contemplation of that family at breakfast any more……" But he did have to return to England, staying in Dover until the Hogarths left Tavistock House where they had been staying and where they had allowed him to pay their bills.

Catherine returned from being with the children in the park to find Charles and his manservant wielding fluffy dusters in their hands. 'Wilkie and I will be doing a play here, now that your "imbecile" parents have removed themselves we can get down to rehearsals.'

What was left to say? He wasn't interested in anything she thought or felt.

'You may say nothing, but I expect every room and everything in it will have to be spring cleaned. Your mother and father have scant regard for my property.'

'My parents and I can do nothing right.'

Henry ran into the room and got hold of Catherine's skirts, looking up into her face he pleaded. '"Aunt Georgie" says I may play now Mama, will you come?'

'Of course, I should love to.' She took him by the hand.

A tense day lengthened into an embarrassing night for Catherine. She and Charles entertained guests. Georgina, John Forster, Francis Beard and Wilkie Collins sat around the table.

The bracelets that were on top of Catherine's arm fell into her soup. She glanced over nervously to Charles who laughed "uproariously, his eyes streaming with mirth". She was clearly self conscious and there was an awkward silence.

The maid stepped forward and coldly spoke, 'may I madam?' She removed the soup, offending bracelet and brought another bowl for Catherine.

Charles ignored the exchange between Catherine and

Anne at the table and addressed the company in general. '"Collins and I have a mighty original notion" to produce a theatrical together.'

'Do you mean a theatrical play?' John Forster showed interest.

'Yes, it's to be set on the ocean wave with sea salts a-plenty, isn't that so Collins?'

'It is indeed.'

'It sounds interesting.' Forster approved.

'I'm sure it will prove so.'

Georgina was enthusiastic, 'I love plays.'

'You're a fun loving creature my dear.' Charles smiled at Georgina, who basked in the approval Charles showed her. The meal continued with Charles not speaking or paying any attention to Catherine until he spoke to her indirectly, 'ladies, do you wish to retire?'

Francis Beard jumped forward to help Catherine remove her chair and leave the table while Charles took away Georgina's chair.

The men lit cigars and sat with their drinks, Charles expanding on his earlier proposal, 'we can do rehearsals here, the rooms are small but we'll manage admirably.'

'Will Catherine wish to have us?' Wilkie Collins questioned.

'Don't concern yourself on Catherine's account, let the matter rest there, I want to accommodate the cast.'

'Good, we'll progress quickly.' Collins lowered his voice, 'I've been thinking, how about strolling around the "Rookeries" tomorrow evening?'

'That would be agreeable.'

The evening continued with 'man talk' until the ladies returned.

# Chapter Eight

The following night Charles and Wilkie wandered among the "Rookeries" frequented by "low women" and their pimps, when a prostitute approached them, 'doing business?'

Wilkie thought for a moment, 'that depends.' He took a drink of opium from a small flask.

'Depends, depends on what? Don't toss me 'round. My favours cost two shillings.'

'Two shillings Madam, it can't be less?'

'A shilling then, that's the best price I can do.' She waited expectantly and then slouched off into the night when she saw there were no takers.

Charles allowed himself a small smile and began talking, '"If the mind can devise anything sufficiently in the style of sybarite Rome in the days of its culminating voluptuousness, I am your man". I'm restless, I can't settle to work here. I want to escape from myself . Wild ideas are upon me of going abroad somewhere and writing. I need a change.'

'Is that possible?'

'It will be, if I make it. Catherine and I are not made for each other and I'm endeavouring to realize my dreams. I've been looking at Gad's Hill and at last I'm in a position to buy. The papers will be ready in a little while and I can make what I hope will be my last move, but for now I must return to the home I have.'

It wasn't long before Charles had the news he wished for. He waved a letter in the air to Georgina. 'It's my "lucky day" Gad's Hill the house of my dreams is to be mine. I have the letter which tells me so.'

'Oh Charles I'm pleased for you.'

'As I knew you would be.'

He stopped, 'but my intelligences tell me you've had a proposal of marriage from Augustus Egg.'

'Yes, that's so.'

'You'll accept?'

'I think not.'

'You mustn't let any considerations for this family stand in your way.'

'I know what I want.'

'Let us hope so. We rely on you, you know we do. Catherine is so ineffectual and Anne Brown leaving us to get married hasn't helped.' He paused. 'I know your parents arrive tomorrow, I shall go out before they come.'

'Poor Charles, we Hogarths are a trial.'

'Tut-tut, you know that isn't true.' He didn't wish to involve himself in any discussions at that moment. He made for his study.

The production of The Frozen Deep in Tavistock House caused an upheaval where there were so many children and adults. New gas lines were introduced to facilitate the lighting effects and Charles spent more money than he intended.

He stood in a doorway of the schoolroom trying to pitch his voice to Georgina, over the noise of hammering, 'is everything alright Georgina?'

'Yes Charles, a little noisy but we're getting on.'

Charles squeezed out of the way as a wooden stage was brought past and in no time at all his guests were seated for the

108

first night of the play. Lines of chairs filled the small space and on them were seated the Hogarths, Catherine, Georgina and the family. Katey was seated next to Charles Alison Collins, (Wilkie Collins brother.) Wilkie Collins, John Forster and Dr.Beard rounded up the numbers. Reporters were squeezed in besides other celebrities.

The small stage had a backcloth of icebergs surrounding two sailing ships. Chinese lanterns were strung out over the boards and shrubs in pots edged the stage.

Charley Dickens junior played First Lt. Crayford and Charles Dickens senior played Captain Helding.

Charles senior began. "'I want you to wait for a volunteer who has just joined us".'

"'A volunteer!'"

"'Yes. He has his outfit to get in a hurry and he may be half an hour late".'

"'It's rather a sudden appointment isn't it?'"

"'No doubt. Very sudden".'

"'And – pardon me – it's rather a long time to keep the ships waiting for one man".'

"'Quite true again. But a man worth having is worth waiting for. He only returned from foreign service".'

"'You astonish me".'

"'I dare say I do. When he presented himself at my hotel and told me what he wanted his words startled me, if I don't take refuge in absence and hard work I am a lost man. Will you give me refuge? That's what he said word for word".'

"'Did you ask him to explain himself further?'"

"'Not I! I knew his value and I took the poor devil on

the spot. The facts speak for themselves in these cases. The old story, my good friend! There's a woman at the bottom of it of course".'

The audience applauded and Charles Alston Collins turned to speak to Katey Dickens, 'it was splendid wasn't it?'

'Yes, indeed.'

'Can we go on enjoying theatre, would you come out with me one evening?'

'I should like that.' Katey warmed to Charles Alston.

Entertaining was lavish after the show and the evening ended between eleven and twelve, after a gigantic supper.

Charles wasn't disappointed when he read the newspaper review on The Frozen Deep. He told Georgina and Katey 'The reviews are "inimitable". They're excellent, excellent.' He laid his paper in his lap. 'We can't surpass what we have done as a family acting together but if we're to go on with the production in a bigger hall to reach more people I must look for such and professional actresses to project themselves. It's no reflection on the family. The Frozen Deep has certainly captured the public's imagination.'

'And Royalty's heard of it too!' Georgina added more to Charles's endorsement.

In the interim, the play was produced in the Gallery of Illustration while Charles sought suitable actresses for an even larger venue. An acting family, the Ternans were thought to be suitable, the mother Frances and the daughters, Maria, Fanny and the youngest, eighteen year old Ellen.

At the same time arrangements had to be made before Walter sailed to India to take up a post with the East India Company.

Yet in spite of everything Charles worked feverishly to bring the play to The New Free Trade Hall. Outside the billboards proclaimed 'The Frozen Deep' while inside the seated audience, mostly in evening clothes waited for the show to start. The larger backcloth with a ship caught in ice was dropped and the Master of Ceremonies came on stage proclaiming, 'tonight it gives me great pleasure to present Mr. Wilkie Collin's The Frozen Deep. As you know friends this is produced by no other than Charles Dickens. The production is based on the ill-fated Franklin Expedition and Mr. Charles Dickens and the beautiful Frances Ternan and her equally delectable daughters, Fanny, Maria and Ellen are your cast. My good people I give you.' He held out his arm and Charles and the Ternans came on stage. Charles bowed and the Ternan girls dropped a curtsy. The Master went on, 'Mr. Charles Dickens and the Ternans. So without more ado we voyage The Frozen Deep.'

The M.C. left the stage and the scene changed to that of a ball where the complements of two ships setting out on the Franklin expedition are taking their leave. The music begins and the dancers take to the floor, the men, debonair in uniform and the women corseted in lavish gowns. Charles partners fair haired eighteen year old Ellen Ternan. Wilkie Collins dances with twenty year old Fanny Ternan and twenty-two year old Maria Ternan is propelled around by Charley Dickens.

It didn't take long to be apparent to all that Charles couldn't take his eyes off Ellen Ternan and Catherine, in the audience could not take her eyes off Charles. Ellen Ternan would be his next temptress; he'd already fallen for her.

Later in the men's dressing room Charles and Wilkie Collins were taking off their greasepaint. 'You were superb Charles.' Wilkie complemented his friend.

'I tried to be.'

'The Ternan's were enchanting; did you know Ellen is only eighteen?'

'Yes I knew that but they are all professionals and quite captivating.'

'Do I detect interest?'

'It's more than that, it's real longing.'

'Well there's a party on after the show, come, she'll be there.'

'I daren't. I will know no peace now that I have set my heart upon such a creature. "I do suppose that there never was a man so seized and rendered by one spirit". The marriage tie chafes.'

'It can only do that if you allow it to get in the way of what you want out of your life.'

'You wouldn't, but I've got to. There are more than enough columnists waiting for a story to spread over their newspaper presses.'

'Poor Charles, you shouldn't bother about the scandalmongers.' He opened the door, 'I'm off. By the way Charles Alston is very smitten with Katey.'

Charles could not mask his sardonic ness, 'I observed your brother was drawn.'

Later that night Charles went to bed with Catherine who lay with her back towards him as he imagined himself sweeping around holding Ellen Ternan in his arms during the evening's production. Neither got any sleep and neither spoke.

It was no surprise to Catherine when Charles let it be known that he was leaving with Wilkie Collins to go on another trip. He was frustrated and wanted to put space between himself and Catherine but claimed he was gathering material for his writing. He did go to the lakes as planned, but a newspaper printed an article announcing that he and Collins had been seen at the theatre where Ellen had been appearing in Doncaster. The facts were in black and white print for all to see.

On Ellen's return to London Charles was instrumental in securing her next part in a theatrical cast. After the booking he wrote the manager of the theatre in the Haymarket thanking him. "I need hardly tell you that my interest in the young lady does not cease with the effecting of this arrangement...." and at the same time sent him fifty pounds. He was becoming close to Ellen and was one of the first visitors to call on her when she came back to the capital. After they had drunk tea, he discussed his part in arranging her affairs. 'I thanked the Manager at the Theatre Royal for his assistance in securing you an engagement.'

'You've given us a lot of help Charles.'

'Consider me your manager.'

'I do.'

Charles kissed her hand and she suggested, 'shall we play cards?'

Charles pulled a face.

'A duet perhaps?'

She went over to the piano and sat down where he joined her. She began to play 'Home Sweet Home'.

Charles sang to the melody, 'be it ever so homely

there's no place like home.' He was at peace with Ellen and resentful of Catherine. His "want of something" ceased to be in Ellen's presence.

Now he felt able to decry Catherine even more openly and as was usual his feelings were committed to Forster on paper. "….Catherine and I are not made for each other… Her temperament will not go with mine….What is now befalling me I have seen slowly coming on, ever since the days you remember when Mary was born; and I know too well that you cannot, and no one can, help me".

He unburdened himself to the de la Rue's in Genoa.

Mr. de la Rue opened the note. He went very quiet and his wife remarked, 'you are giving your letter a lot of attention dear.'

'It's from Dickens, such a sad note.' He read "'I don't get on better in these later times with a certain poor lady you know of, than I did in the earlier Peschiere days. Much worse, much worse! Neither do the children, elder or younger. Neither can she get on with herself or be anything but unhappy. She has been excruciatingly jealous of, and has obtained positive proof of my living with, at least 15,000 women of various conditions in life since we left Genoa". He goes on to say he doesn't know what the girls would be without Georgina.'

In the London clubs and elsewhere, a lot of conjecture continued about the state of the Dickens marriage. In one such club George Hogarth sat with a colleague commenting, 'Dickens has been the subject of most of our conversation.'

'He certainly has. He provides the ammunition himself. His writing of letters will be the death of him. He reveals all.'

Hogarth paused. 'He's also had the impertinence to say "the skeleton in my domestic closet is becoming a pretty big one...."'

'Does he mean Catherine?'

'I guess he does.' George fumed.

'He hasn't helped matters by keeping company with Wilkie Collins.'

'He certainly hasn't. The two of them are always off to the continent. Collins's mistress must be very understanding.'

'She must be. They're saying Collins takes enough laudanum to kill six men!'

'He's not a well man. I've heard he takes it to kill the pain. He could kill himself and of a certainty Dickens will go too far one of these days.'

'He's done it already. One of our number said he "admired Charles Dickens as a writer but despised him as a man" and another notable of ours aired the view that "Dickens is evidently not liked".'

'So what he is up to is anyone's guess!'

Tavistock House was an unhappy place and it wasn't the right time to have visitors to stay but Charles had invited Hans Christian Anderson to visit and the writer was eager to come to England. Charles and he had a lot in common. Hans too, had wanted to be an actor and worked hard at his writing. Charles was enthusiastic about Hans's ability, writing him, "do not stop writing because we cannot bear to lose a single one of your thoughts. They are too true and simply beautiful to be kept in your own head".

When Hans arrived the family discovered his English was poor, but he did charm them all by his cutting out of paper, beautiful "little" figures and designs. On one occasion as he lay in the garden with Charles nearby he became very upset at the newspaper he was reading. '"My work has been attacked".'

'"Never allow yourself to be upset by the papers, they are forgotten in a week and your book stands and lives".'

'"It is hurtful".'

'It truly is, but its life.'

Hans collected himself, 'will you come to the theatre this evening?'

'I'm sorry Anderson, I have a prior engagement but Catherine will accompany you.'

Catherine went to the theatre and the two enjoyed their evening.

However the general consensus in the Dickens household agreed that Hans's failing was he tended to overstay his welcome. By the time he departed, some five weeks later, Charles was bracketing him with his dislike of Wordsworth. When the visitor did depart Charles quickly fixed a note over the mirror in the room where Hans had slept. "Hans Christian Anderson slept in this room for five weeks – which seemed to the family AGES".

Mamie passed the open door and looked in, 'is he really gone?'

'Yes the ugly duckling has waddled off.'

'Katey and I call him "Thebonybore".' Father and daughter laughed together.

Leaving his hosts Hans gave his visit and the situation in the Dickens home his consideration; he could not but see that Catherine had "a certain womanly repose" and had felt sadness as he saw her crying when coming out of a room with her mother. He viewed Georgina as, "piquant but not kind".

# Chapter Nine

Charles sought for a solution to his marital impasse. The answer he came up with was to direct their newly returned, married servant Anne to bring it about.

Catherine sat combing her hair in the master bedroom when there was a knock on the door. She called out, 'come in.'

Anne Cornelius came into the room and stood at Catherine's side to say, 'Ma'am I've had a note from the master.'

'A note?'

'Yes Ma'am.'

'Go on.'

'He's told me to close the doorway off between the dressing room and this room and to have the recess filled with shelves.' She stood waiting.

'I see Anne.'

'Yes Ma'am.' When the servant saw Catherine would say nothing further she left the room.

Catherine's lip trembled and she couldn't stifle her sobs. He'd made his move at last! No more pretence. He'd shown her up before Anne, but that wasn't a new thing. However the timing of Charles's next move was wrong for he entered the room and Catherine threw her hairbrush at him. 'You're less than a gentleman. You wrote Anne to tell her to carry out your instructions. You didn't have the stature to tell me yourself. You are beneath contempt. I've put up with much for the sake of the children but I can't stomach any more.'

Charles retreated and almost walked into Anne

Cornelius. His voice had an explanatory tone as he spoke, 'Anne, I haven't had the chance of thanking you for making all the arrangements I asked of you and making sure Mrs. Dickens received my note. You'll see for yourself how much your presence is needed.'

Anne nodded her head and Charles went to his study and stayed there.

Later in the day as Catherine sat in the drawing room looking into space there was a tap at the door and her mother came in dressed in outdoor clothes. She sat beside her daughter, instantly seeing that something had upset her. In the background hammering could be heard.

Catherine's mother took her hand, 'whatever's the matter?'

'Charles has written Anne telling her to have the door between the dressing room and our bedroom blocked up so that I may not enter; the workmen are doing it now.'

'He's written to a servant with an instruction like that! Even for Charles Dickens he's exceeded himself! He's a puffed up serpent. Where is he?'

'I think he's in his study or he might have gone out with his literary friends.'

Her mother shook her head in disbelief.

'I've thought a lot about Charles and I understand my position in a way I never did before. I see ours was a marriage of necessity on his part. He hated his own family and he saw Papa, you, and we girls, were happy. I was an escape from his situation but now I'm not necessary. Charles has fame, a home and the children. I did think he loved me but there were always others, even if sisters.'

'Don't torture yourself Catherine, you have borne his children. That must mean something.'

'It means he always had a 'husband's rights' but he no longer even needs those.'

Her mother sighed. 'I can scarcely believe he's changed so much. At first he showed us nothing of the man he has become.' She gave Catherine an apologetic look. 'It seems a small matter that I came about, but your father and I wondered if Miss Coutts could be of help in placing Edward in a "situation". A word from her could secure his future.'

'I'll write her mother, although I cannot promise a result but she's always been gracious in the past, I'm sure she will strive to help my brother.'

Hours later when her mother left for home she penned her parent's requested letter and then went to Charles's study, opening the door to enter and stand in front of him at his desk.

He looked up. 'The children will stay with me and I will make provision for you elsewhere.'

'But Charles the children need me too.'

'Your sister will look to their needs. When I was but a small boy I had no one to give me counsel.'

She ran from the room and when she did meet Charles in the days ahead there were searing arguments, one of which arose because he had learnt of her writing to Angela Coutts regarding Edward. He was livid and wrote the bank heiress asking her forgiveness for Catherine's approach. When he later came face to face with her in the corridor he stopped her, 'you should not have made such an overture to Angela.'

'Charles, you allowed her to pay for Charley's school fees and she helped with Walter's career. In fact she assisted in finding employment for your brother as an engineer. You know that's the custom in society.'

'I know we're no longer "man and wife", we are disassociated.'

The altercations went on relentlessly, so much so, that one night Charles walked miles to Gad's Hill, the house he hoped to buy, in the dark. His equilibrium had deserted him, he considered giving more readings, he thought of re-visiting America and then the whole situation took another downward spiral.

Georgina came into the drawing room looking for Catherine. She held a modestly sized parcel. 'The jeweller's just brought this.' She handed Catherine a very small brown paper package.

Catherine took it from her and walked over to a table where she put it down and untied the string. Within the layer of brown paper and tissue rested a finely worked filigree bracelet. 'It's not for me,' she stared at it intently. 'The jeweller has sent it to the wrong person, have it returned.'

Georgina came over and took the bracelet from Catherine. A look of irritation crossed her face. 'I wonder who it was meant for, it's lovely.'

*It's not only me he makes unhappy, it's Georgina too.* What is he up to? She guessed the "keepsake" was intended for the young actress he'd played opposite in the Frozen Deep. He hadn't hid his admiration.

'Can't you guess?'

'I can't.' For once Georgina looked uncomfortable.

That evening Catherine confronted Charles. 'You bought jewellery for Ellen Ternan and they delivered it here to me. She's eighteen years old. You're old enough to be her father.'

'More pettiness, you know I often buy items for the cast after a play.'

'I know that but you're in love with her. Everyone's talking about you, because you talk about her. I can't think why you married me. I've begun to believe you never loved me, that you had the idea of having a settled home of your own because the home you had was never so. You needed a wife and I was in your view, the correct age and from the right background. I've tried to be what you wanted, I've tried to be a dutiful wife and I've borne you children. I can't be as Mary or Georgina. I've seen the way they've responded to you. Georgina sees you as a man of "genius", but I wonder – how have you seen them?'

Charles waved his arms in the air and strode around the room. 'There you go again with your jealousy.'

'Aunt was right when she said you had changed into a "spoilt child of fortune". You want Ellen Ternan.'

'Madam you are quite mad.'

'You would wish it was so.'

'Do you remember the compact we made many years ago? Well perhaps it's time you called on Ellen Ternan if you think I love her.'

Charles stormed out to walk to Kensal Green Cemetery and stand holding onto Mary's headstone. When he came back he had another blazing row with Catherine when he told her she **should** go and see Ellen Ternan and apologise for thinking ill of her. In the early hours of the morning he took opium to get some sleep.

The next day Katey put her head around the door to see her mother "seated at the dressing table" sobbing while trying to tie her bonnet in a bow. She came in, her voice concerned. 'Mama?'

Catherine tried to stop crying.

'Whatever's the matter?'

"Your father's asked me to go and see Ellen Ternan" and apologise for thinking ill of her.'

"You shall not go". Katey stamped her foot. 'He can't ask you to do that.'

Catherine attempted to dry her eyes. 'I must. I'm not mistress in my own home.'

Katey spoke bitterly. 'We must all do as father wishes. He doesn't wish me to marry Charles Alston.'

'I know dear, but you're entitled to some other life than this.'

'I must escape from father. I've been giving it a lot of thought. I'll marry Charles Alston. I have respect for him. He's one of the kindest and most sweet-tempered of men. I may not love him but I must leave this "unhappy home".' She looked about her before scurrying along the passageway and Catherine's emotions seesawed.

Days ago her parents had called on her. Her father had asked her to send for Georgina. When she came into the room Anne had been summoned to ask Charles to join them. Coming into the drawing room where they were he looked surprised yet he must have heard her mother and father arrive. Of late he had avoided herself and her parents but they were all together in one room. Her father looked Charles straight in the eye and shocked them all. 'I believe Catherine has grounds for divorce because of incest with Georgina.'

Georgina appeared stunned.

Charles waited. "Have you finished"? You dare to come to my own house and accuse me of such vile acts against your own daughter. Your lies are grossly false......' He defended himself strenuously but Catherine was in such a state she remembered little except that he turned on her parents. 'Do you **want** Georgina to have to have a virginity test to prove she is Virgo Intact a? **Is that what you want? Is that your wish?'**

His voice changed for Georgina. 'My dear I must ask something frightful of you. You have heard it has been said improper conduct has taken place between us. We both know it's a fabrication by those who would do me harm but will you submit yourself to an examination to prove it's not the case?'

'I see I must.'

'Your loyalty does you credit.'

He stormed out of the room and Georgina followed.

Catherine's parents, as long as daylight lasted, tried to comfort her then a cab was called and they were driven home through the murky streets.

Their daughter knew now the marriage was ended. Charles had been offended and he never took slights lightly. The matter wouldn't end there. She only had to wait. She understood if incest were proved, it would finish him as a writer. He had enough critics already. Were he imprisoned it would not be in a debtors' prison but a criminal penitentiary.

Charles realised he needed to understand the new Divorce Act and very quickly asked Forster, always his friend and mentor to write to Charles's solicitor to learn the grounds needed to obtain a divorce. He also revealed what he was thinking to Forster regarding Catherine. "It is all despairingly over…A dismal failure has to be borne and there's an end…."

Very soon after Catherine called at her parent's home and they told her they had come to the decision that it would be a detrimental step as parents to sanction the idea of a virginity test.

She sought Charles out. 'Mama and Papa don't think it advisable that Georgina is examined,' she stood in front of him apprehensively.

'It's well that you all see sense.'

She waited for him to go on and when he didn't she left the room.

In the days ahead Charles did nothing but search for a way out of the predicament he found himself in. He went to the drawing room where he knew he would find Catherine doing her embroidery. She tearfully paid attention.

'There are things we must discuss. We must find a solution to our situation. We could lead separate lives but appear as a married couple at dinner parties held here. Or you could go abroad and live alone. Another idea would be to live in the country while I am in town or vice versa.'

'I'll have to discuss it with my parents,' Catherine wound her hair around her finger anxiously.

'Can you stop doing that?' Charles looked at her with distaste, 'why do your parents have to be brought into this?' He didn't wait for an answer. 'Georgina has expressed a wish to stay here with the children.'

'You have it all planned Charles.'

'Our affairs and that of our children must be put in

order.'

'Your affairs and the children's must be arranged only to your satisfaction, as well as Georgina and Ellen Ternan.'

'Georgina and Ellen don't enter into this.'

Catherine's laugh sounded cynical, even to herself. 'If Ellen Ternan doesn't matter, Georgina does, she's going to stay here while I'm made to leave, no wonder people talk.'

Charles stormed out into the night to find his way to St. Paul's Cathedral where he sat on the steps his eyes fixed on the night sky. Thinking of Catherine he regretted he "had ever fell her way".

Catherine's parents did not share the same sentiments as Charles and thought his ideas for the ending of Catherine's marriage were not what she deserved. Catherine herself thought them unworkable and so Charles and she were forced to meet again for a solution.

Charles sat writing as he waited for Catherine to come into his study. She seated herself at the opposite side of his desk while he adjusted his cuff links. 'As you or your parents reject the idea I put to you regarding a separation settlement, I have another possible solution. You could possibly be set up in a house elsewhere with four hundred pounds yearly and your own brougham. I've asked Forster to act for me in regard to the matter and Lemon or Evans will act for you.'

'I must speak to Mama and Papa.'

'It doesn't concern them.'

'It concerns me and I need some counsel, just as you once did.' She went from the study to her parent's home to tell them what had been proposed.

Catherine's young family were all very upset at their

mother being made to live alone. In addition, their father had always ruled his household and those in it and they knew his present position wouldn't change, thus for the time being, they all obeyed their father.

Twenty-one year old Charley knocked on his father's study door, 'come in, I wanted to see you.' his father instructed.

Charley sat on the seat indicated.

'You're aware that your mother and I are having difficulties?'

'Yes Sir.'

'I will be at Gad's Hill soon and I propose that the family move with me.'

'What of mother?'

'She'll have alternative arrangements.'

'I see.'

'It's for the best Charley.'

'Yes Sir, goodnight Sir.' Days later, even after a lot of deliberation, Charley couldn't accept his father's actions and knew that like himself, not one of his brothers or sisters could begin to see where the present situation would take them all.

It seemed an age since their father had left any of them a note saying "quite slap up" when he inspected their drawers each day. Charley realised there was little "brightness" in his father's world.

# Chapter Ten

The separation was put in hand and Catherine, her mother and father sat with Mark Lemon and Frederick Evans, associates of Charles.

Mrs Hogarth grumbled, 'Dickens only cares about himself that's why he wants to keep out of the law courts. He's already had much experience in them through his writing.'

Frederick Evans sought to pacify her, 'I understand this is all very painful Madam but we must try to come to some agreement. Charles has suggested that Catherine might possibly live abroad in a warmer clime, he's anxious to find a solution to satisfy both parties.'

'Rumours are rife about him – and not for the first time – but as Georgina again is the subject of one of the stories it concerns our family. Did you know they are saying Georgina has had a child in Calcutta by him? I must say I do not agree about the stand Georgina has taken. It's imprudent for her to stay in the same house as Charles Dickens, especially at this time. Catherine should never have married the man.'

'Madam I pray you, do not upset yourself so. We must mend this affair for Catherine's sake, we must consider her.'

Catherine sighed, 'it seems I have little or nothing to do with it. It's what Charles wants; I'm to have none of my children with me.'

'It's unthinkable that our daughters should be in such a position.' Mrs. Hogarth paused for a moment only. 'And what about Ellen Ternan?' Catherine's mother couldn't help herself.

Mark Lemon ignored the remark regarding the actress and instead went on, 'believe me Madam we are not without sympathy and anything Mr. Evans or I myself can bring about will be done.'

'Catherine cannot go abroad to live in isolation and she must have a more adequate settlement.' The arguments went on for some time.

Mark Lemon straightened up. 'Should we leave it there for the present? We'll pass on your sentiments to Charles.'

A huffy Mrs. Hogarth puffed, 'very well.' The meeting was over.

Elsewhere Charley was about to have a discomforting encounter with his father. Gauging it an appropriate time he knocked on his study door.

'Come in.'

'You got my note father?'

'Yes Charley I did and although I cannot understand why you feel it's your duty to live with your mother, I can see you have your reasons.'

'I will still see you and my family.'

'Of course.'

Charley stood awkwardly waiting but no more was said. He knew by his father's voice that he was offended.

Catherine tried to hold her life together in some pattern of normality. Mrs. Hogarth now came to stay with her at Tavistock House and Charles moved out to his offices at Wellington Street North.

Thinking of the Hogarths he could not "bear the contemplation of their imbecility any more".

A broken Catherine wrote Angela B.Coutts. "One day though not now, I may be able to tell you how hardly I have been used".

Tangled lives went on and with her mother Catherine went to arrange flowers on Mary's grave. She pulled the dying blooms from the vase and looked at them. 'We didn't bring these.'

'Charles' her mother said. She took them from Catherine's hands, gave them a withering look and threw them away.

'He still calls her "my dear girl". If she had lived I don't know what he would have done.'

'The situation was not of your making. Your father and I did not see any harm in her buying him the inkwell and could not protest when he bought her a desk. She put him on a pedestal as a writer and we know he craves adulation.'

'That's true mother, it's something I didn't give him.'

'You gave him a family.' Mrs. Hogarth patted Catherine.

'And I sometimes wonder how much he wanted them.'

'He has been an impossible man to please.'

In their absence George Hogarth called on Charles and faced him out in his office. Charles gave him no chance to speak and immediately challenged him. 'I heard more lies today and unless your family do not sign a retraction of their accusations I won't continue with any increased settlement for Catherine.'

'We're not the instigators of this misery.'

'Please leave, I have writing to do. I must provide a settlement for your daughter.'

George Hogarth did not move immediately although he had been dismissed and Charles disregarded him as he drew pen and paper to him and began to write a hard to understand letter to Burdett Coutts explaining his marriage. "I believe that no two people were ever created, with such an impossibility of interest, sympathy, confidence, sentiment, tender union of any kind between them, as there is between my wife and me". George Hogarth threw him a scornful glance and found his own way out. Charles wrote on, "Her mind has, at times, been certainly confused.... If the children loved her, or ever had loved her, this severance would have been a far easier thing than it is. But she has never attached one of them to herself, never played with them in their infancy, never attracted their confidence as they have grown older, never presented herself before them in the aspect of a mother. I have seen them fall off from her in a natural – not *un*natural – progress of estrangement and at this moment I believe that Mary and Katey (whose dispositions are of the gentlest and most affectionate conceivable) harden into stone figures of girls when they can be got to go near her, and have their hearts shut up in her presence as if they closed by some horrid spring. It is her misery to live in some fatal atmosphere which slays every one to whom she should be dearest".

The present state of affairs continued to chafe and wound. Catherine had been correct in her assumption that Charles would seek to absolve himself from all blame in the break-up of their marriage. The absolution came in the form of an article printed in Household Words which lay on her lap. She read it twice.

"Some domestic trouble of mine, of long standing, on which I will make no further remark than it claims to be respected, as being of a sacredly private nature, has lately been brought to an arrangement, which involves no anger or ill-will

131

of any kind, and the whole origin, progress, and surrounding circumstances of which have been, throughout, within the knowledge of my children. It is amicably composed, and its details have now to be forgotten by those concerned in it....By some means, arising out of wickedness, or out of folly, or out of inconceivable wild chance, or out of all three, this trouble has been the occasion of misrepresentations, mostly grossly false, most monstrous, and most cruel – involving not only me, but innocent persons dear to my heart...I most solemnly declare, then – and this I do both in my own name and in my wife's name – that all the lately whispered rumours touching the trouble, at which I have glanced, are abominably false. And whosoever repeats one of them after this denial, will lie as wilfully and as foully as it is possible for any false witness to lie, before heaven and earth".

He was blaming her parents for everything that had happened. He was sharpening his words to wound. Catherine had always followed Charles's writings and was an informed reader of newspapers but at this point she questioned whether she should look at any other articles in the press. She did continue to read on, largely because Charles was no longer speaking to her and she could not be aware of what he was claiming in her name if she failed to read what he published and so when another diatribe came into her hands, even more personal because he questioned her mental stability, she read the print.

Tuesday, May 25, 1858.

"Mrs. Dickens and I have lived unhappily together for many years. Hardly any one who has known us intimately can fail to have known that we are, in all respects of character and temperament, wonderfully unsuited to each other. I suppose that no two people, not vicious in themselves, were ever joined together, who had a greater difficulty in understanding one another, or who had less in common. An attached woman servant (more friend to both of us than a servant) who lived with us sixteen years, and is now married, and who was, and still is in Mrs. Dickens confidence and mine, who had the closest familiar experience of this unhappiness, in London, in the country, in France, in Italy, wherever we have been, year after year, month after month, week after week, day after day, will bear testimony to this.

Nothing has, on many occasions, stood between us and a separation but Mrs. Dickens's sister, Georgina Hogarth. From the age of fifteen, she has devoted herself to our house and our children. She has been their playmate, nurse, instructress, friend, protectress, adviser and companion. In the manly consideration towards Mrs. Dickens which I owe to my wife, I will merely remark of her that some peculiarity of her character has thrown all the children on someone else. I do not know - I cannot by any stretch of fancy imagine – what would have become of them but for this aunt, who has grown up with them, to whom they are devoted, and who has sacrificed the best part of her youth and life to them.

She has remonstrated, reasoned, suffered, and toiled, again and again, to prevent a separation between Mrs. Dickens and me. Mrs. Dickens has often expressed to her, her sense of affectionate care and devotion in the house – never more strongly than within the last twelve months.

For some years past Mrs. Dickens has been in the habit of representing to me that it would be better for her to go away and live apart; that her always increasing estrangement made a mental disorder under which she sometimes labours – more, that she felt herself unfit for the life she had to lead as my wife, and that she would be better far away. I have uniformly replied that we must bear our misfortune, and fight the fight out to the end; that the children were the first consideration, and that I feared they must bind us together "in appearance".

At length, within these three weeks, it was suggested to me by Forster that even for their sakes, it would surely be better to reconstruct and rearrange their unhappy home. I empowered him to treat with Mrs. Dickens, as the friend of both of us for one and twenty years. Mrs. Dickens wished to add her part, Mark Lemon, and did so. On Saturday last Lemon wrote to Forster that Mrs. Dickens "gratefully and thankfully accepted" the terms I proposed to her.

Of the pecuniary part of them, I will only say that I believe they are as generous as if Mrs. Dickens were a lady of distinction and I a man of fortune. The remaining parts of them are easily described – my eldest boy to live with Mrs. Dickens and take care of her; my eldest girl to keep my house; both my girls, and all my children but the eldest son, to live with me, in the continued companionship of their aunt Georgina, for whom they have all the tenderest affection that I have seen among young people, and who has a higher claim (as I have often declared for many years) upon my affection, respect and gratitude than anybody in this world.

I hope that no one who may become acquainted with what I write here, can possibly be so cruel and unjust, as to put any misconstruction on our separation, so far. My elder children all understand it perfectly, and all accept it as inevitable. There is not a shadow of a doubt or concealment among us – my eldest son and I are one, as to it all.

Two wicked persons who should have spoken very differently of me, in consideration of earned respect and gratitude, have (as I am told, and indeed to my personal knowledge) coupled with this separation the name of a young lady for whom I have a great attachment and regard. I will not repeat her name – I honour it too much. Upon my soul and honour, there is not on this earth a more virtuous and spotless creature than that young lady. I know her to be innocent and pure, and as good as my own dear daughters. Further I am quite sure that Mrs. Dickens, having received this assurance from me, must now believe it, in the respect I know her to have for me, and in the perfect confidence I know her in her better moments to repose in my truthfulness.

On this head, again, there is not a shadow of a doubt or concealment between my children and me. All is open and plain among us, as though we were brothers and sisters. They are perfectly certain that I would not deceive them, and the confidence among us is without a fear".

Catherine later learnt Charles had sent the letter with the stricture. "You have not only my full permission to show this, but I beg you to show, to anyone who wishes to do me right, or to anyone who may have been misled into doing me wrong".

There was no question of it being a private letter, it was for his readership. Charles wasn't writing in such a vein without a veiled purpose. Why? Weren't things bad enough? Hadn't he already said he would never forgive her mother and sister "living or dead"? She fretted. Was he trying to destroy

135

her? He was using the same language as he had done years earlier. Yet he had written her "I earnestly hope all unkindness is over between you and me".

In the following weeks Catherine's parents did all they could to help her carry on in a situation which daily became more untenable. They visited her as much as they could in Charles's absence and were scandalised at Georgina's continuing assertion to take Charles's side.

Catherine's tears often came, it was as though Georgina had stepped into her own shoes, yet she herself was still in the house! Meals were taken in silence or on a tray and each avoided the other.

Catherine needed to unburden herself to those she could trust, she couldn't engage the public as Charles did. She wrote her aunt. "I have been told that he has expressed a wish that we should meet in society, and at least be on friendly terms....Surely he cannot mean it....I feel that if I were ever to see him by chance it would almost kill me".

She sat with her father and mother and they cast around in their minds as to what could be done. One answer they came up with and agreed on was to appeal to Angela Coutts. She had some influence on Charles and they hoped she would listen to Catherine and understand her unenviable position. Charles had left home, what was in his mind? Perhaps Angela Coutts knew more than they did, perhaps not. A lot of Charles's secrets were for his men friends only.

Catherine arranged that her mother and self call on Angela Coutts, whose dismay at the affair made her quickly write to Charles on Catherine's behalf, but the letter only served to incense him more.

For his part Charles thought endlessly about the problem of extraditing himself from the marriage without dishonouring himself.

He had a lot to think on. He had joined the Garrick Club a long time ago but for different reasons over the years, had resigned, only to be re-admitted. Now the current story in the club was that Thackeray, a contemporary of his, had corrected a fellow member who had heard Charles was separating from Catherine because of an affair with his sister in law. Thackeray had said he believed the trouble to be an actress and when Charles heard of the conversation he stopped speaking to Thackeray. He also cut himself off from Mark Lemon and Fred Evans as they had refused to print his *Personal* statement in *Punch.*

There were stinging reports in more than one newspaper. The Liverpool Mercury observed. "This favourite of the public informs some hundreds of thousands of readers that the wife who he has vowed to love and cherish has utterly failed to discharge the duties of a mother; and he further hints that her mind is disordered....If this is 'manly consideration', we should like to be favoured with a definition of 'unmanly selfishness and heartlessness'".

Charles was half deranged, fearing the public would desert him and fail to buy his books.

The worsening situation was continued as Charles went on believing that Mrs.Hogarth and her eldest daughter Helen were spreading more stories about himself and Georgina. He wrote to his solicitors demanding that they obtain a promise from the Hogarths to say nothing more on his affairs. The family again denied they were the perpetrators of the scandal and Charles presented them with an Appendix to his 25<sup>th</sup> May letter to the effect that they would remain silent. The proviso was that if the document remained unsigned, the increased separation of £600 per annum for Catherine would not go ahead. Key sentences in Charles's document were. "We solemnly declare that we now disbelieve such statements. We know that they are not believed by Mrs.Dickens, and we pledge ourselves on all occasions to contradict them as entirely destitute of foundation".

Catherine despaired when she read the paper and turned to her mother. 'Mama this is all too much. Charles has never made a secret of the fact, even to me, that he admired pretty women. I'm agreeing to what he proposes and that is an end to it. I'll agree his terms. I would go as far as to say that Georgina led him on but it could be Ellen Ternan he is now paying attention to. Charles is keeping her and her family; I have it on good authority.'

'That man is a viper, has he said anything about Kate's wedding?'

'He's told me he will not allow me to attend.'

'He exceeds his authority, he's a puffed up python.'

Reluctantly the Appendix was signed by Mrs. Hogarth and her daughter and grudgingly Catherine was allowed access to her children.

On being told of Catherine's decision to accept Charles's terms Mark Lemon and Charley were relieved at her decision. They had urged her to settle the matter.

The document was attested and Catherine left home, Charley joining his mother some weeks later. She moved to a smaller place in Gloucester Crescent but not before Charles had called at the house to pick up a forgotten book and summonsed her into his study addressing her immediately as she stood in front of him. 'The children must not come into contact with your mother or Helen.'

'But they may stay with Georgina, because she takes your part.'

'Leave Georgina out of this.'

'And why is that? She seems to have an opinion. She's quarrelled with all her family because they dare find fault with you.'

'You have no perception of the situation.'

'That's the point. I have every perception of what goes on in your mind. You can't control or hide your feelings. It's you who make them public. I've seen a published letter of yours that says I have a "peculiarity of character" and I occasionally labour under a "mental disorder". What are you thinking of? It's you who are disturbed. You've long been the cause of gossip but I never understood why as I do now.' She paused. 'You will be angry to know I've given Katey and Charles Alston my blessing, if they're ever allowed to marry.'

Charles was clearly taken aback by Catherine's outburst and left her standing alone in his study.

He re-assured himself that he had succeeded in removing her from her home and alongside Mamie, had put Georgina in charge as his closest confidant. It was she who wrote to Maria Winter. "By some constitutional misfortune and incapacity, my sister *always* from their infancy, threw her children upon other people".

And it was Charles who replied to Angela B.Coutts when she suggested Catherine might attend her daughter's wedding. "It is simply impossible that such a thing can be. That figure is out of my life for evermore (except to darken it) and my desire is, Never to see it again".

Such a situation called for more letter writing on all sides. Catherine wrote her aunt. "….you will understand and feel for me when I tell you that I still love and think of their father too much for my peace of mind….I trust by God's assistance to be able to resign myself to His will, and to lead a contented if not happy life, but my position is a sad one, and time only may blunt the keen pain that will throb in my heart, but I will indeed try to struggle hard against it".

But worst of all, she lived precipitately with the knowledge that when she was ill Charles had tried to have her committed to a lunatic asylum but the doctor had refused. What manner of man was he? Why did he choose to remove her in such a way? She had striven to be a good wife and mother.

Yet it was not to be a peaceful existence in the Dickens household without Catherine. Charles called the family together. 'I've something to say to you. I forbid you to be in the same room as your grandparents or Aunt Helen. I'll tell Charley of this. "I positively forbid any one of you children to utter one word if you are ever brought into the presence of either". I charge you "immediately to leave your mother's house and come back to me" if such a situation should arise.' He went on. 'The same goes for Mark Lemon and Frederick Evans, you are not to associate with them.'

His quarrel continued with Thackeray. He recoiled in horror when remembering he had wept in the Athenaeum Club when being quizzed about the state of his marriage. The spectators there must have had a fine time that evening! At his expense! He guessed Thackeray would have commiserated with Catherine at a dinner party they'd both attended. He still felt anger at Thackeray and compared his background with his own. Thackeray Senior had fathered a black daughter and had been a wealthy Anglo-Indian. What a beginning! Thackeray was quite unlike himself, who was the son of a down-and-out-clerk.

Thackeray himself had loved a married woman; gambled and had been born with a silver spoon in his mouth, he had been to Charterhouse and Cambridge and had contracted a gonorrhoeal infection.

Charles hesitated during his reminiscing. Like Thackeray, he was a man of the world, he had his own "small malady" and it meant he had to show restraint and curb his inclinations. He shook his head, why did Catherine know him so well? She'd accused him of frequenting "low places" saying people were talking, why was she always right? He'd done his best for the prostitutes, but in what manner had they rewarded him?

Time went on and he made many enemies as his treatment of Catherine became known. Some of his acquaintances refused invitations to his home. Leading newspapers continued to condemn him for his stance. He felt estranged from a lot of people. He became less involved with Angela Coutts and her charity work; after all she had seemed to take Catherine's part. She'd even invited Catherine to make her home with her before the separation was agreed! His mind went back over the years. When he'd campaigned on the need for good sanitation because of frequent outbreaks of typhus fever and cholera and had said so in a revolutionary manner Angela had wrote him in alarm. She wasn't always prepared to back his causes! Friends!!!

# Chapter Eleven

Charles knew full well that Catherine had never been happy at his absences as he pursued his interests but now with his new found liberty he could spend time and money as he wished. One such cause he chose to further was the Great Ormond Street Hospital for Sick Children. However, even if time would allow, his money commitments were increasing. He had to pay Catherine to have a separate existence and Nelly and her family were being maintained as well as his own children and his siblings. As always he turned to Forster for advice on the question of undertaking more readings, but when it didn't concur with his own ideas, he dismissed the recommendations.

Although he rejected his mentor's advice on some counts he still sought his opinion on other matters. One quandary he could not make up his mind on was whether he should lease Tavistock House to the Ternans. This time he was persuaded from taking such a course of action but instead took a lease for them on a property in Houghton Place.

From Gad's Hill he planned a reading tour to take him all over England and as he travelled, threw himself into his many engagements believing that the scandal had made little or no difference to the public's attendances at his shows.

But his lisp did still give him some concern and in order to achieve the best possible delivery he turned to Ellen Ternan.

They sat facing each other late one afternoon. A confident Ellen spoke, 'recite the vowels after me, A. E, I, O, U.'

Charles carefully pronounced, 'A, E, I, O, U.'

'Again Charles, and pay attention to your pronunciation.'

He put even more effort into his speech, 'A, E, I, O, U.'

She listened carefully. 'Yes that's better. We'll get on with Plato's Gorgias.' She handed Charles a small book, which he opened at the bookmarked page and read.

'Calicles.' "Your arrival Socrates, is the kind they recommend for a war or battle".

'Socrates.' "Do you imply that, in the proverbial phrase, we are late for a feast?"

'Charles you're becoming more distinct. You must go on practising, the more the better.'

He leant over and kissed her on the cheek, 'I promise you I shall.' He leant back in his chair. 'I've something I wish to ask you. Can we be as "'man and wife" not good friends?'

Ellen didn't immediately grasp what Charles meant then she chose her words carefully, 'may I think about it Charles? I didn't expect such a proposal.'

'Take the time you need my dear, but I promise you, you'll not want if you come under my protection.'

They sat together in the dusk, not thinking to light the candles.

Georgina put her head around the door with her outdoor clothes on and hastily explained, 'I'm calling at the butchers and bakers.'

Neither answered and as she set off down the street her thoughts ran riot. Was this friend more to Charles than she'd been? It certainly looked like it. Since she had come back from abroad Charles had seemed to keep out of her way. He was unfailingly courteous but it was almost as though he were afraid of her. But if she could fall pregnant, this new woman could! She knew now that Charles would not wear the label incestuous, which a liaison with herself would cost him, but what of the actress?

She completed her purchases and hurried back to Gad's Hill recalling that Catherine had found both Mrs. Ternan and her daughters "too familiar" when rehearsing at Tavistock House. As she stepped along the street she was not to know Ellen was already securing her future.

'Charles, your earlier question – the answer is yes.'

'Dear girl, you'll not regret it. You'll never want.' He kissed her. 'May I give you a pet name? One that is used for you already.'

'If it suits me' she waited for him to speak.

'It's Nelly.'

'Just Nelly? That suits me.'

He took her in his arms.

Very shortly after Fanny and Maria Ternan transferred the lease of Houghton Place which Charles had secured for them to Nelly.

There was a great deal Charles did not wish to become public knowledge and so his concern was to destroy the many letters he had written and received over the years. Behind Gad's Hill in a field he had a bonfire lit and his family carried out basketfuls of correspondence for the flames to destroy. Charles gathered up the fragments that blew away and Katey asked him, 'ought we not to keep some father?'

'No, we're sweeping the old life away, Tavistock

House is sold now and we must press on. "We should always remember that letters are but ephemeral: We must not be affected too much by those who praise us or by others written in the heat of the moment. Would to God every letter I had ever written was on that pile".'

Charles believed he had been liberated but that was not quite so. He still had difficulties. He had to deal with the death of his brother Alfred and his daughter had not given up the idea of marrying. She sat in the garden at Gad's Hill with her fiancé, discussing their wedding. Charles Alston accused, 'your father is opposed to our marrying.'

Katey pulled a face. 'It's no use to pretend otherwise, he's so dominant, but I'm determined I won't be ruled, at least in this. He makes us all unhappy at home. He won't allow Mother to attend our wedding.'

'He's taking the wrong course regarding your mother. She deserves our respect, she should be visited. After all, your father isn't going to know – and if he were to find out it's not his concern. We should act kindly towards her.'

'You're a good man Charles Alston.' Katey kissed him.

'In any case you're in Gloucester Crescent every week when you go to your music lessons with Mamie, you could call in then.'

Katey hugged him and despite her father's objections she married her red haired Charles Alston during a very small ceremony where there were games and arches of flowers in the garden.

Charles strolled around the lawn with his friend who remarked, "a lovely wedding Charles".

'Yes "the whole affair is a great success SO FAR".'

Catherine was excluded from the wedding by Charles.

Whilst the young couple were on honeymoon in Nice Mamie went to Katey's bedroom. When she entered she found her father on his knees crying with his face buried in Katey's wedding dress. She stood there and when her father realised he was being watched said emotionally, '"but for me, Katey would not have left home".'

Charles's life had changed. Catherine was gone, he had brought that about himself, Katey had married and the only person who remained constant was Georgina, running Gad's Hill with Mamie but her health appeared to be faltering. Charles described it as "degeneration of the heart" but he did wonder if she was seeking his attention and so there was no rest for him. His relationship with Nelly was now unsettling him, more than his feelings for Georgina, which alternated between love and fear.

His life was not straightforward. He had to attend to the affairs of his "mother, who was left to me when my father died (I never had anything left to me but relations)...." She "is in the strangest state of mind from senile decay and the impossibility of getting her to understand what is the matter, combined with her desire to be got up in sables like a female Hamlet illumes the dreary scene with a ghastly absurdity that is the chief relief I can find in it". She tried him sorely before passing on.

Undertaking more readings did not assuage his distressed mind, it served to physically wear him out. Life was unknowable and in time, his adversary Thackeray, passed away but not before he and Charles were reconciled. Charles mourned him at the graveside and shook the hand of Mark Lemon, another long estranged friend.

Saddest of all, Frank, Charles's brother, had gone out to join Walter but on arrival in Calcutta was told he had died a month earlier, leaving debts to be taken care of. The news reached Charles on his fifty-second birthday. Calcutta and all its associations, what would another year bring?

In order to achieve the seclusion he wished, he rented a chalet in Condette, France and Nelly with her mother, were the main inhabitants. He arrived on one of his frequent visits and sat outside in the garden with the two women. Mrs.Ternan busily doing crochet got up and went into the house for more yarn to work with and Charles took his chance to speak in private. 'Nelly, there's a matter I wish to discuss with you, a matter it would be imprudent to write of, I find it difficult.'

'Charles?'

'I cannot concentrate on my work. Not being with you and at other times being with you and yet not being as "man and wife" is making me restless.'

Nelly saw she could no longer hold back and must accommodate Charles. 'Mother is going off tomorrow to make a call. I know you've had to wait for us to be together and it's a short time but it's all I can do with mother here. I'm sorry it's got to be this way.'

'Nelly, my love.'

Mrs. Ternan came back into the garden and they talked theatre, 'The Frozen Deep' and theatrical scandals.

The following day a carriage collected Mrs.Ternan and Charles with Ellen went to her bedroom. In bed together, he whispered, 'for a day my terrible sadness is banished, this is how I wish us to be, "man and wife".'

'I've never been a wife Charles.'

'My love', he took her in his arms.

He stayed for as many days as he could in the presence of Mrs.Ternan and then took Nelly on a last stroll. 'It has "brightened" my days being here.'

She slipped her arm through his.

'I wish we could stay here forever and let the world say what it wants.'

'Our lives are not so simple.'

'My life has become a trial and I must go back tomorrow.'

'Yes you must.'

He kissed her.

Charles's snatched visits to France were as frequent as he could make them but there were always commitments at Gad's Hill.

Later in the year when he made the crossing from England to rejoin Nelly he could see something was different. She was tense and when her mother left them alone her words cascaded, 'I'm afraid. I'm going to have a child,' she searched his face. 'Are you angry?'

'Angry at you?'

'Angry at us.'

'If there's any anger, it's at life.'

'I've told my mother and sister. They're going to help me, to arrange it all. Fanny's going to find a midwife.'

Charles visibly overwhelmed, pledged. 'I will of course, send you money. There is a great deal to plan for.' Taking her into his arms he held her close, 'it's impossible to stay long, my presence will be missed if I don't return to Gad's Hill but I do yearn to be close to you, especially now. Is your mother upset about what has happened?'

'She hasn't said a great deal, while Fanny has said more. I have only just told them and they've been very quiet, except that they did promise they would help me. But they're both adamant that no-one should know.'

'Of course my love, that's what we all wish.'

Charles did not see much of Mrs.Ternan as she pleaded "vertigo" and kept to her room and Fanny was spending a few days away. He lingered as long as he judged safe with his "sick friend" and on leaving vowed he would visit her as soon as he could. Each took courage in the fact that plans had been made as Nelly awaited the birth.

On one such visit he explained to her. 'If I thought otherwise that I was placing you in the care of your sister I could not bear these enforced partings but you must have privacy for what's to come. She's so protective of you and your reputation I feel nothing but gratitude for her care. While you're not with me I'll exercise my mind to make arrangements for you when you return.' He patted her hand. 'I'll plan things in the proper way so that no finger of reproach can be pointed at you.' Once more he had to return to Gad's Hill, his absence would be noted if he were missing.

In the chalet Fanny talked pointedly to Nelly. 'You must stay here, you cannot go anywhere until after the birth.'

'I know Fanny. Charles is giving me money for everything.' Nelly strove to keep the irritation from her voice.

'Well it is **his** concern, no-one must know. Charles isn't the only person involved in this. What of Mama and myself? As for the birth, I've learnt of an old midwife in the next village, I'm sure she'll be able to look after you properly. She's delivered babies many times.'

'Would it not be better to go to a lying in hospital?'

'Babies are delivered all over the world by midwives.'

'But I don't know her.'

'You'll meet her. Depend on it, you'll have this baby.'

The days ahead were anxious for Nelly. She was afraid of having the birth. She feared for what the world would say if she was found out. Her reputation would be ruined and Charles wouldn't be happy if his book sales dropped. Her mother and sister were not hiding the fact that they were growing tired of the situation. She sat at a desk chewing the end of a quill pen, not knowing what to write until she began, 'Dear Charles....'

It seemed a long time later when her mother and sister were on either side of the bed and she had just given birth. The midwife held a stillborn boy. She gave the infant a smack on the back and the child didn't stir, she did this again, without result. Watching this smacking of the baby, Nelly began to cry. Fanny went to the midwife and took the baby giving the boy another slap on the back. They looked at each other, realising he would not live.

'We did everything we could.' Fanny protested.

'I've seen it done as the midwife did it.' Mrs. Ternan agreed.

'Give me my baby.' Nelly cried. 'I should have gone to a lying in hospital.'

An exasperated Fanny retorted. 'You wouldn't have had a secret you would have had a scandal.'

In the following months Charles made crossings to France to the "sick friend concerning whom I am anxious". He would tell his family and others, I will "vanish into space for a day or two".

Eventually one of their most painful episodes passed for the lovers and there was now no reason why Nelly and her mother shouldn't travel back to England. Returning from Condette in a first class carriage of the Folkestone train Charles felt at ease with Nelly beside him. Mrs. Ternan sat very comfortably on the other side of the carriage with the train travelling at twenty-thirty miles per hour. Passing an embankment, Charles exclaimed at everything as it flashed by. 'What a revolution, we are doing nearly fifty miles per hour and when I travelled in stage coaches while I was a young reporter we were fortunate if we travelled fifteen an hour.'

Mrs. Ternan was agreeably impressed, 'times have certainly changed.'

'They have indeed.'

'I like this way of travelling, it's exciting.' Nelly pressed her nose against the window.

Charles suddenly became downcast. 'What lies ahead isn't exciting, if we were going back at all I wish it were to produce another theatrical, Wilkie has a wealth of ideas.'

They sat watching the fields slip by.

Just in front of the locomotive the engine driver saw a straight run ahead of him yet there was a lookout with a red flag on the track trying to wave the train down. In the very far distance he could just glimpse a gap in the rails which made him apply his brakes frantically. Whistling to the guards the air was filled with deafening blasts and the metallic sound of screeching brakes and hissing of escaping steam. Their carriage swayed erratically from side to side. Charles and the Ternans gripped their seats until they were thrown into a corner and the train abruptly ground to a halt.

Mrs. Ternan cried out "my God" while her daughter screamed.

Charles managed to calm them down and seat them in a corner. 'Compose yourselves ladies; I'll see what has happened.' "Pray don't cry out". He tried for some time to open the door but it had become jammed. His eyes searched the carriage and when they came to the window he lowered it with difficulty and climbed out to extradite Nelly and her mother. He made sure they were ushered away from the site then found out their carriage was the only one remaining on the tracks. The others had crashed down onto a river bed where wounded people lay. He helped the train porters and gave brandy from his flask to the injured. At the end of the day he retrieved the manuscript he had been working on from the compartment but could not locate Nelly's belongings. This loss caused him to write to the Goods Office in Charing Cross where two porters were dealing with the lost luggage.

'There's a letter from Charles Dickens 'ere asking if we've found a gold watch chain with a smaller gold watch chain attached, a bundle of charms and a gold watch- key and a seal engraved "Ellen". Have you come across any of them? He says they got lost on the Folkestone-London train.'

'Not yet, A' haven't.' The second porter shook his head. 'It sounds as though he does keep company with that Ternan woman after all!'

After such an event Charles was unwell but his first

thoughts were for Nelly. He called his young manservant to his side. "Take Miss Ellen tomorrow morning a little basket of fresh fruit, a jar of clotted cream from Tuckers and a chicken, a pair of pigeons or some nice little bird. Also on Wednesday and Friday morning take her some other things of the same sort – making a little variety each day".

His worries escalated, twenty year old Alfred had migrated to Australia trying to evade his debts and causing Charles annoyance and embarrassment. Lying in his sickbed Charles's sentiments were; "He had brought up the largest family with the smallest disposition for doing anything for themselves"! He thought further, he hoped his charity in asking Charles Alston to do the illustrations for Edwin Drood would not be misplaced, hopefully it would be a wise move. Charles Alston was reckoned to be one of the best illustrators but he questioned the outcome, he had chosen him in an effort to please Katey.

When he had settled his home life he returned to his private world. He took Nelly house-hunting as soon as he recovered enough and circumstances allowed. They chose a small cottage in Slough near to the house he had already rented for herself and her mother. They strolled through the rooms.

'Do you think it will suit?' Charles prodded a window frame.

'I'm sure it will. I adore it.'

'It needs refurbishing but it has quite a feeling of refinement. I approve of it, it should answer well.'

'It's charming.'

He kissed her. 'Shall we take it then?'

'Yes.'

They concluded their inspection and Charles locked the door behind them. They walked along the path arm in arm for a few paces until Charles stopped, took out his hip flask and had a drink. Nelly put on a wide brimmed hat and pulled it well down, to walk separate from Charles into the village where they came to a very small office on the High Street. They entered and a bell tinkled over the door. The proprietor looked up. 'Was the property suitable Sir?'

Charles laid a bunch of keys down on the counter. 'Yes indeed.'

'You are taking it?'

'I am.'

'What name shall I put?' As the Proprietor's pen was poised to make an entry in his book it made a blot.

'"Charles Tringham".'

'How do you spell that?'

"T R I N G H A M".

'I shall attend to it Sir.'

'We'll call again.'

They left the office to go to the property he had rented for Nelly and her mother in Church Street as the Staplehurst crash continued to reverberate. Charles was asked to attend the inquests but he declined, not wishing his name to be mentioned in connection with the affair.

What he could not decline to do was to set out on another reading tour to cover his expenses, even if his health was severely compromised after the crash.

# Chapter Twelve

Before he departed for America he sought out his doctor. 'Beard, I'm undoubtedly out of sorts.'

His friend took his pulse. 'On the low side.'

'It always is.'

'Well it shouldn't be; rest more man.'

'I would, but I haven't got time.'

Beard examined his ankles. 'You won't have any more time if you don't stop driving yourself and another thing, I suggest you get yourself a walking stick, get the weight off that foot.'

Charles took part of the advice and bought a blackthorn walking stick for the tour but disregarded the recommendation to rest. This course meant that it also went against Forster's counsel not to embark on such a trip and led to another falling-out between the two.

He was upset by all the gossip. Disturbingly the ghost of Seymour, who he thought had vaporised into the ether, now materialised in the form of an article written by Seymour's son claiming that Charles had used his father's work. Notwithstanding his relationship with Catherine he wrote her a note asking her to back his rebuttal on the circumstances of his only meeting with Seymour in Doughty Street and as though the phantom of the illustrator wasn't enough to disturb him, his daughters, Mamie and Katey were also drawing detrimental attention to themselves. Many disparaging remarks levelled at Mamie and Katey were because they chose to be with Charles and the more moneyed exciting life he had to offer while their mother lived in straightened circumstances and did not have her family around her.

Drained and exhausted Charles prepared for his tour. Coming out of the hall one day he met Katey as she came through the front door greeting him, 'good morning father.'

'Good morning my dear.'

'Is Plorn (Edward) here?'

'Yes, he's playing cricket at the back of the house.'

'May I take him to see Mama?'

Charles visibly shrank. 'You may, but don't let him eat too many ices and sweets, it doesn't agree with him and if he's taken out onto the streets into "Little Italy" see he has none of that ice cream the Italians are making in their back yards.'

'Yes father.'

He hobbled off, leaning heavily on the walking stick he was now forced to use and Katey sought Mamie out. Finding her in her bedroom she entered it and stood expectantly. 'I'm going to make a point of going to see mother today, are you coming?'

'I can't. I've promised to help Georgina.'

'We haven't seen her since she left.'

'I know.'

'Perhaps you'll come next time.'

'Perhaps.'

Katey closed the door softly and she and Plorn crossed London to find Catherine sitting doing embroidery in her small Gloucester Crescent home. She looked up, 'Plorn and Katey: how lovely to see you both.' Plorn went and stood by her side and she kissed him. 'I shall ring for refreshments. Cook has some of your favourite biscuits Plorn.'

'He must not have too many sweetmeats Mama.'

Mother and daughter exchanged a look.

'I understand dear.' She patted the seat beside her. 'Now what have you been doing Plorn?'

'Well Mama, I'm practicing my cricket very hard and I found some frogs playing in the garden.'

'How lovely, you're doing exciting things.'

'Yes Mama I am, but I should like to stay with you. What will you do when we go away? Will you be lonely?'

'I shall miss you Plorn but I'll look forward to the next time I see you again. It's so good to have you here.'

'Charley looks after you, doesn't he Mama?'

'He does indeed; Charley is very good to me.' Catherine put her arm around the standing Plorn. 'Would you like to get a jigsaw out?'

Plorn went to the cupboard and brought out a puzzle to begin playing with it.

'And what about you Katey?'

'Well I'm still practising cooking. Charles Alston appreciates my doing it.'

'And how is Charles Alston?'

'He's not been so well Mama. He's had so many colds and aches and has been sick a great deal.'

'This city, the "Great Oven" as your father calls it, isn't good for our well being. In fact capital cities are quite similar in that respect. You must look after him and care for him.'

Katey lowered her voice. 'I mean to mother but father's angry at Charles Alston. Charles Alston cannot do the illustrations for father as he promised. It's just too wearing for him and father cannot understand this at all. He seems to think all illustrators are troublesome.'

'It's that business with Seymour's son. Try not to heed him dear. He just doesn't understand illness.'

'And that's not all. Father is insisting Charles Alston is dying.'

'That's not the case. None of us know when our time comes.'

'You're right mother, of course, you're right.'

'I am on this occasion.' She smiled her attractive smile. 'Now tell me about Plorn's schoolwork, is it satisfactory?'

'It is Mama, only you know Papa, he expects everyone to strive so.'

'Yes I know how it is, but we mustn't talk of your father, it causes pain.'

Katey seemingly embarrassed, shifted on her seat. 'Mama we should go, we can't be too long and it takes a long time to get back. We'll come again on anothe occasion.'

'I look forward to it my dear.' Catherine stood up to say goodbye to them both and without delay they travelled through London to arrive at Gad's Hill.

On their arrival Plorn ran off and Katey went to her father's study. 'He's home father.'

'Yes I can see he must be. I'm leaving in the morning to do more readings.' He picked up his papers and continued reading.

Katey saw she'd been dismissed and realised since their Mama had gone their father was even more removed from them all. She made her own way out.

Charles dropped the paper he was reading. His family

159

gave him cause for concern and annoyingly Catherine had asked him to go and visit her. However he would delegate Georgina to refuse her a visit. It was all very distasteful, Catherine had always been clinging.

When Catherine received Georgina's letter, written per pro Charles, she thought of the many times it had been her duty to answer his letters.

The one redeeming feature in Charles's life was that at least he and Nelly were still together and it gave him a good feeling to know it was he who had introduced Nelly's sister Fanny, to his friend Trollope, who she had later married.

As he deliberated on the course he would take in the future he made the decision to call on Nelly. He could not plan his life without her. They sat alone in the cottage and he took her hand. 'I'm banking money for you; it will be called the "N Trust". I want you to be financially secure, especially if I go to America. I don't want to go without you, but I can't see how it can be possible for you to accompany me, even on the pretext of visiting relatives. I must devise some way of letting you know whether to come and join me or not and I have settled on a way of telling you. I will send a telegram to my old friend Wills and he will forward it on to you. If I send you a telegram which says "All well" it means you come but if I send you a telegram which says "Safe and well" it means you don't come. I will send my letters the same way, as you well know, people are watching us.'

'I understand Charles.'

'I shall miss you Nelly.'

'I'll miss you too Charles, but I know you won't forget me and the telegram will soon come to tell me what to do.'

'You may be assured of that my dear and should you want for anything Forster "will do anything for you if you want anything done".'

'I'll be alright Charles.'

He sat back in his chair. 'I'm heart sick of all my commitments, of all the readings, of hotels, of being at Gad's Hill when I would rather be here. Perhaps we could find something more than you have here, something closer, something more discreet.'

'Whatever you think Charles, but there's something I've been meaning to say. I can't bear you children as Catherine did. It just isn't possible.'

She had never heard such sadness in his voice. 'If that's so, I must accept it.'

'It's for your reputation, as much as my own.'

'True, I am hunted down by the press. When Catherine and I married I had regard for her, in fact I could have thought it was love but now I've feelings unlike any other and they make me sorrowful. It would be better for my peace of mind to not return to you but I can't carry that out, I am drawn as a moth to a flame.'     He sighed. 'Is this Fanny and your mother's idea: that we should not be together as "man and wife"?' Nelly didn't answer. 'What happened over the birth of our child caused us both the utmost grief and I thought at the time that your sister was acting in our interests! It "is impossible to swallow" what she has allowed to happen. She is "infinitely sharper than the serpent's tooth," I will say no more on the matter.'

'It was not all Fanny's decision. She and mother were worried about what people would say about me and that's why they found a local midwife. It causes me pain to say I can't go on like this. If I were as a wife to you again I could fall pregnant and I can't keep disappearing. Mother and Fanny feel such situations can't be kept secret for ever and I feel mother is tired of living in isolation.'

'My dear girl, you're upset at all you have gone through, please re-consider.' A smitten Charles took hold of Nelly's hand. 'I too have had to make adjustments in my private life but nothing makes a difference as to how I feel about you, I can't stop loving you.'

'Charles.' She touched his hand.

'And I fail to understand why your sister has changed her view so drastically.'

'Mother and Fanny feel this way protects your reputation and my own and I see they have a point.'

'I've no choice but to leave things as they are for the present. My feelings won't change and I'll continue to provide for you. If I can't be your husband, I'll be your brother.'

'I'm glad you see it that way.'

Reluctantly Charles returned to Gad's Hill in order to search for a larger house for them. They settled on a two-storied villa with a garden surrounded by fields in Peckham.

His growing-up family found it hard to understand where and when he would be at home but a time of definition came. He would go to America but before he could begin to take the matter seriously there were urgent matters to put in order. Charley had received help from Angela Coutts to invest in a paper-mill enterprise but had gone bankrupt. Charles avoided possible embarrassment to the Dickens name, to a degree, by setting Charley to work for himself and drew comfort that the debtors' prisons had all but disappeared from the London streets.

Before boarding the ship dinner speeches had to be made, theatres attended and arrangements made. Nelly was travelling to Italy at the same time with her mother to stay with her sister Fanny and brother-in-law.

Catherine enjoyed lessened circumstances yet she had many friends and coming from a literary family, enjoyed going to the theatre. One evening she went with a friend to such a performance. Sitting waiting for the cast to appear on stage, she was startled to see Charles enter with associates and take his seat in a box opposite to where she sat. There was no mistaking him, flamboyant waistcoat and buttonholed dinner jacket. He combed his hair. His immaculate turn-out proclaimed him a "gentleman about town".

She was inordinately grateful that just at that moment the lights were extinguished. Ordinarily she would have been at his side but publicly she sat apart from him. The tears ran down her face, she didn't make a sound but her cheeks were moist. He had loved her. She had the letters to prove it. They were addressed to "My dearest life". "Dearest Darling Pig" or "Mouse". She made up her mind to show them to Angela Coutts. What would Angela think of her? Angela had never had a man laying down ultimatums. She resolved that at the end of her life she would deposit Charles's letters to her with The British Museum. He hadn't always been as he was now.

She was brought back to reality by her friend touching her on the arm, "let's go home dear". The audience sitting in the same row were forced to stand up during the performance but they didn't seem to mind the premature exit. Catherine's friend later described her sentiments to her husband in private. 'I took her home to Gloucester Road and "I thought I should never be able to leave her; that man is a brute".'

In her lone life Catherine also had to come to terms with the fact that she had asked Charles for help sorting out her affairs. His answer, when it became known to her stung. "It is my fixed purpose (without any abatement of kindness otherwise) to hold as little personal communication with her as I possibly can".

She believed Georgina had written the missile at Charles's behest and felt humiliated at the blunt refusal.

For his part Charles was gratified when an invitation came from America asking him to give a series of readings. In fact a committee of private "gents" in Boston were ready to deposit a guarantee of £10,000 in advance at Coutts bank to lure him over the Atlantic. His family and doctor were against the idea, they had seen him wan and worn out but the lure of money drew him back to the States. Before he left England he wanted to be sure of the reception awaiting him and sent his manager, George Dolby to cross the Atlantic. What he heard told him a public were waiting who would prove receptive.

He travelled to Liverpool with Katey, Mamie, Georgina, Charles Alston and Wilkie Collins and others to spend the night in a hotel. Next morning he left on board the Cunard mail steamer Cuba with two of his staff, arriving in America to find his four month planned reading schedule punishing. It was a matter of urgency when he telegraphed Nelly 'Safe and well'. It was impossible for her to join him and hard for him to wait to get back to her. He contented himself by sending her a cheque for one thousand pounds.

Arriving in Boston he was re-assured to learn from Dolby that all the tickets for his first reading were snapped up. Queues snaking around the buildings when the tickets became available were lengthy and Charles wrote back home of his reception. 'That the appreciation shown was "beyond description or exaggeration".' One of the readings he gave on the tour had been A Christmas Carol and a Mr. Fairbanks who was head of a large factory had listened and took it to heart. That year instead of working Christmas Day the factory was closed and every factory hand received a turkey.

Charles's tour had been a triumph but he was ready for home. His catarrh impeded his reading yet he carried on, "I read as I never did before, and astonished the audience quite as much as I did myself. You never heard such a scene of excitement". He sustained himself on – "a tumbler of new cream and two tablespoons full of rum at 7 o'clock before rising. At twelve noon a cherry cobler and a biscuit. At 3 o'clock (dinner-time) a pint of champagne. At five minutes to 8 o'clock an egg beaten up with a glass of sherry". At times he drank strong beef tea, soup or an alcoholic drink.

Arriving home in England the houses leading to Gad's Hill were bedecked with bunting. Gad's Hill itself was covered in flags but as soon as it became possible he went to Peckham to be with Nelly. He drew her to him. 'It's so good to be with you again. I was saddened not to have you by my side in America.'

'I was sad not to be there.'

'It had to be that way.'

'I understand. I really do.'

'Dear girl. That is part of your charm. You know I

want you.'

She nodded. 'It's not possible.'

Defeated, he stayed some days, before travelling on to Gad's Hill, Georgina and family. This was a period of uncertainty for him, spending weekdays in London and weekends at Gad's Hill.

Plorn at sixteen years of age had to be found suitable employment. Charles considered Australia, believing it would be advantageous for him and discussed the matter with Georgina, 'should I send him "to journey so far"?'

'I believe so Charles, look at the success you've become.'

Charles didn't look wholly convinced but paid attention to her words and the boy was seen off at Paddington Station en route for Western Australia to join his brother Alfred. On the station Charles shed tears and Plorn looked away but not before Charles gave him a letter to carry telling him, "I was not so old as you are now when I first had to win my food and to do it out of this determination; and I have never slackened in it since".

Days before Plorn went away he went to see Catherine to say goodbye. When he took his leave she immediately wrote him so that the letter would be waiting for him in Australia. She bathed the page in love. "I miss you most sadly, my own darling Plorn…"

Mamie, Katey and Georgina also added their letters to Catherine's for his arrival in Melbourne. Katey asked Plorn to remember them "and above all dear Papa, and make his name more honoured than it is already".

Shortly afterwards Charles wrote him. "Never abandon

the wholesome practice of saying your own private prayers, night and morning. I have never abandoned it myself, and I know the comfort of it". It was a time of sorrow for Charles, Fred his brother died and the only "bright" light on the horizon was Henry studying at Trinity College.

Within a very short time Nelly ceased to be at his Peckham address so much, causing him a "terrible sadness" but she did still travel with him on his next relentless reading tour in their new strained relationship of "brother and sister". This particular set of readings resulted in Charles not being able to get out of bed.

Dr.Beard was sent for and stood over him. 'I thought I told you to stop any readings.'

'You did Francis but I've a need to do things.'

His doctor grimaced as he examined his ankles and took his pulse. 'How've you been?'

'I can't sleep as I used to and I'm faint and giddy. Sometimes I've trouble with my words.'

'Well it's up to you.' Beard packed his bag and made to leave. 'I'll let myself out. You must stop; I can't guarantee your health otherwise.'

Charles did try to follow the advice given by his doctor but he found it impossible to do less and as Georgina was unwell he took her to Dublin for a "change of air", reiterating his usual words, "the longer I live, the more I doubt doctors".

In her father's absence Katey took the opportunity to visit her mother. She was concerned regarding her husband's health and knew her father would not have been the person to discuss the matter with.

# Chapter Thirteen

Catherine patted the chair beside her. 'Katey my dear sit beside me, I'm delighted to see you, tell me how Charles Alston is.'

'He's not been well Mama, always sick. I'm afraid he's losing hope over doctors doing anything for him and father has no patience with him. Charles Alston can't help being ill.'

'No I'm sure he can't, the poor man would not wish it.'

'I'm sure father cannot forgive Charles for admiring Pre-Raphaelitism. He hates anyone or anything to do with the painters. He just can't see that others can have a different point of view.'

'I fully understand Katey. I've grown used to your father's ways.'

'You more than anyone.'

They sat in a comfortable silence then Katey changed the subject. 'But how are you Mama?'

'I'm well enough. A friend and I have been to the theatre recently and enjoyed ourselves and I've had a very welcome distraction - I gave a children's party, but that's enough of me. Have you any other news?'

Katey spoke diffidently, 'I know we agreed not to discuss father but I feel I should tell you I've heard a rumour that is saying Ellen Ternan has had a child who died. I would rather you heard it from me than anyone else.'

'I'm not surprised. He's had so many infatuations, Mary Boyle, Christiana Weller and Maria Winter. I'm very tired of them all.'

'So you must be.' She sought for the right words. 'I feel I've not done enough for you and Mamie is feeling that way too. She feels she hasn't visited as she should.'

'My dear no-one can change my position and what should I do without you? Tell Mamie I would love to see her whenever she chooses.'

Katey took her mother's hand, 'I'll tell her mother, she'll welcome such news.'

Catherine nodded her head and went to the bureau bringing a letter from it. 'This has come from dear Plorn. It's a "bright" letter but reading between the lines I believe he wants to come home.' She handed it to Katey who read it and handed it back.

'It would seem so Mama.'

'He seems so far away.'

Their thoughts were interrupted by a knock on the front door and Katey answered, bringing her grandmother, Mrs.Hogarth into the room. Katey kissed her and there was warmth in her voice as she exclaimed, 'this is nice, I'm seeing everyone today.'

Mrs. Hogarth took off her bonnet and cape to sit down. She gasped, 'the rumours, and I'm sure they are true, are saying Dickens sent that Ternan woman and her sister and mother abroad, with letters of introduction and money no doubt. Supposedly one young Miss is learning to sing! And the other sister! Well it's anyone's guess! And I've heard Dickens is in a rage because a policeman questioned the Ternans. He believes they're being watched to find out about their domestic arrangements and wants the policeman dismissed, he doesn't want anyone to know who pays the bills! He won't get the police to apologise for thinking ill of the Ternans!'

'Grandmamma, please try not to think about it, it will do no good. You know father will have his way.'

'He's fallen out with Wilkie Collins again,' Mrs. Hogarth sat tight lipped.

'That's because father is insisting to everyone that Charles Alston is dying. Naturally that isn't what Wilkie Collins wishes to hear or I for that matter. You know how forceful father can be. He believes I have a "dreary unfortunate fate" and won't be persuaded otherwise, but it doesn't help matters.'

There was a pregnant silence broken by Catherine. 'Your father probably blames me for your marriage; I did give you my blessing.'

Katey's grand mamma's words were heartfelt as she broke her silence of a minute or so. 'We all did, you had to get away from the man. Your father isn't always right in his assumptions. In fact he's often very wrong.'

'I know grandmamma. I'll continue to look after Charles Alston.'

'Of course you will dear, no-one doubts it.'

Katey stood up and turned to her mother, 'I must go now Mama, I've been away from Charles Alston long enough. I'll be back as soon as I can.' Kissing both women, she took her leave.

A little time passed and Charles deemed it wiser to be more stationary and compose again, to this end he threw himself into writing The Mystery of Edwin Drood. His "little country house" in Kent became his refuge with its flag fluttering overhead.

During this period Katey arrived for a short stay and it was planned that Mamie would accompany her when she returned home. One evening after dinner, Charles together with Georgina, Mamie and Katey sat in the newly built conservatory at Gad's Hill, he lit his cigar quipping. "Well Katey you now see POSITIVELY the last improvements at Gad's Hill". He waved his hand to indicate the glasshouse, everyone laughed and Georgina stood up.

'I think I'll go upstairs, I've letters to write.'

'I'll turn in too, I'm tired.' Mamie yawned.

Aunt and niece left and Charles and Katey remained sitting.

'There's something I've been meaning to ask you about father.'

'"…. Tell me all about it".'

'I've been thinking. Do you think it a good plan if I consider acting? I've been offered an engagement should I decide to take the step.'

'I don't see that for you Kate, it's scarcely a profession. It may be one day, but not at the present.'

'You enjoy it so. I thought you would be able to give me an objective view.'

'I have my dear, I have. "You are pretty and no doubt would do well, but you're too sensitive a nature to bear the brunt of much you would encounter. Although there are nice people on the stage, there are some who would make your hair stand on end. You are clever enough to do something else" and there are those in audiences who are completely immune to an actress's sensibilities. Nelly had to endure some of that.'

'You know I have no concept of money father but I do

171

know we need it, Charles Alston is not earning.'

'Don't fret Katey, "I will make it up to you".'

She spoke uncertainly, 'I've sold one of my pictures that I painted.'

'Capital, you'll be a recognised artist yet. I trust so.'

She got up, 'I've kept you late enough.'

'Stay Katey, I've got things to stay, I'm getting tired. Edwin Drood has been slow in coming but I trust it will prove a success, "if please God, I live to finish it".' He touched her arm. '"I say if, because you know my dear child, I've not been strong lately". I'm glad I've left London for Gad's Hill. I've abandoned many things and there's a matter I wish to speak of, I need to tell you, Nelly did have a child but it didn't survive.'

Katey couldn't answer and they sat for many minutes while they both tried to come to terms with what had been said.

Charles took the initiative, 'do you remember the old days?'

'When Plorn always wanted to be carried on your shoulders?'

Charles nodded. '"I wish I had been a better father and a better man". I regret parts of my life. I acknowledge your mother was right in her assumption that I've been driven to write and never to enter the Marshalsea's gates again.' His voice lowered. 'The debtors' prisons are all but gone.' He had to acknowledge that Catherine knew him so well, why had he used her so? The word 'desire' came to him and he quickly pushed it to the back of his mind.

They talked on until three in the morning and then quietly climbed the stairs together.

When it came time to leave Charles didn't offer his cheek to Katey to be kissed, he kissed her and when she left him something told her to "go back". She did so and never saw him alive again.

A day passed and Charles helped Georgina drape some Chinese lanterns in the conservatory. They were about to sit down for dinner when she became conscious that his colour had faded and he was unwell, 'Charles, are you ill?'

'"Yes, very ill - for the last hour".'

'Let me send for a doctor.'

'Not yet, I want to walk in the lane or go to London this evening.' Suddenly he grew rigid and Georgina went to him.

'"Let me help you to your room so that you might lie down".'

'"Yes, on the ground".'

She lowered him gently and he slumped to the floor. Running to bring his young manservant she ordered, 'take the pony and go and get the doctor, the master's very ill, hurry.' She ran back to Charles and stayed with him until the local man was brought.

'How long has he been like this?'

'About an hour.'

'We'll make him comfortable – a bed – can you arrange it?'

Georgina left the room and re-appeared with the manservant dragging a sofa with him, Charles was lifted on to it.

'We've done all we can, we must wait it out now. Send telegrams to his family and Beard.' He thought for a moment, 'yes, that would be best.'

Georgina hurried away and the doctor took Charles's pulse and stood over him. He sank into a chair and the clock went around, seven o'clock, eight o'clock. The night passed slowly until a very concerned, Katey and Mamie arrived with Georgina.

Katey murmured, 'can we do nothing?'

'Not a great deal, see he is comfortable and warm,' the locum advised.

Francis Beard came through the door, took Charles's pulse and looking at his ankles said, 'we must keep him comfortable. I think it best to have another opinion besides ours, I suggest Russell Reynolds he's known to be a good man.'

'Send a telegram.' The local doctor consented to another opinion.

Ellen Ternan was sought. She remained in the wings until the last while Catherine was quite alone.

Charley came and with Francis Beard stood over Charles who was watched over through the night. They all took turns to place hot bricks at his feet because they were so cold. But at 6 o'clock his breathing ceased and his own "Battle of Life" was over, in more ways than one. When he had written his "The Battle of Life" in 1846 it had been rejected by The Times and Thackeray as being in bad taste – the theme had been a tale of two sisters loving the one man. That story had a happy ending whereas Charles's did not.

After the death Katey discussed with Mamie what had been said by their father to her before he died. She told of how their father had talked and talked. *How* he talked until three in the morning. 'I know things about my father's character "that no one else ever knew; he was not a good man, but he was not a fast man, but he was wonderful! He fell in love with this girl, I did not blame *her* – it is never one person's fault. She flattered him, he was ever appreciative of praise - and although she was not a good actress she had brains which she used to educate herself to bring her mind more on a level with his own. Who could blame her? He had the world at his feet. She was a young girl of eighteen, elated and proud to be noticed by him". 'No matter who father had married the outcome would have been the same, for he "did not understand women". It would not have been possible to eradicate one "fault" from his make up to leave him the "uncanny genius" that he was.'

'I'm glad you've shared all this with me Katey. I know that if father were ever to say anything about his affairs, it would be to you. Are you going to see mother to talk to her?'

'I'm compelled to.'

'I'll go another day. I just can't face up to it at the moment.'

Catherine had no knowledge of what was taking place at Gad's Hill and went to see a new shop opening that she hoped would carry all the latest in threads. As she went along her eye caught a poster nailed to a door, 'Dickens is dead'. She leaned against a crumbling, sooty wall and then made her way home to sit in her cape and bonnet. She sat there for a long time until Katey made her anticipated painful visit to her.

Katey could see at a glance that her mother knew. Her words were gentle, 'you know?'

'Yes, I saw it on a notice. When did it happen?'

'At 6 o'clock. We thought it too soon to come and this

175

morning has been frantic.'

'He didn't suffer?'

'No, he just went to sleep.'

'I see.'

They sat in the small parlour, Katey striving to ease her mother's distress. 'Try to remember mother that father did say, "I wish I had been a better father and a better man".'

'That doesn't mean he was thinking of me. Ellen Ternan was always first in his thoughts. She was probably with him at the end.'

Katey took hold of her mother's hand. 'Mother, don't torture yourself so. He was not himself.' "If my father had lived, he would have gone out of his mind". In a way he acted like a "madman". He told me that Ellen Ternan had a "resultant child who died in infancy".'

Catherine drew back. 'It had to be.' She chose her words carefully. 'Dearest daughter, it's everything to me that you're the one who's come to me to tell me all this and comfort me. I'll try to remember what you've said. I didn't realise how our lives would be shaped by money and the debtors' prison. He was ever driven to write, the spectre of the Marshalsea haunted him.

He came to not need me. In fact I don't know if he knew himself who he needed or wanted. Georgina was to him what he wished her to be and I think he must have been to Ellen Ternan what she wished him to be.'

Catherine picked up Charles's photograph in a gilt standing frame, sorrowfully she asked, 'do you think he was sorry for me?'

'Mother that last night we talked until three in the

morning but it was impossible to know what he really thought at the end, he wasn't himself. It's certain that the accusations made against you by father were untrue and he strove to keep the younger children in ignorance. He was like a madman when you left home. The "affair brought out all that was worst in him. He didn't care a damn what happened to any of us. Nothing could surpass the misery and unhappiness of our home". He just "did not understand women".'

She went on, 'I've been trying to make sense of what has happened but I found "I told only half the truth about my father and a half-truth is worse than a lie, for this reason I destroyed what I had written. But the truth *must be told* when the time comes – after my death". Gladys Storey has listened to the story and she will give an account of it, though whether she will be believed or not, I cannot say.'

'I too have been thinking on those lines and have decided to give my letters from your father to The British Museum after my death.'

'We are both thinking the same.'

They sat in the half light, reflecting on his "Battle of Life" lost.

Nine years later in 1879 Katey brought Georgina to see her mother who was dying from cancer. Catherine, always the gentlewoman, forgave her sister for the less than sisterly actions.

Katey now often sat with her mother and Catherine asked her to look in a drawer and bring out a bundle of letters. With them was a locket, carrying a likeness of her husband and a lock of his hair. Resting her hand on them she said '"give these to the British Museum – that the world may know that he loved me once".'

Katey promised her mother and with Catherine's death the artefacts were given to the British Museum with the proviso that they were not shown for thirty years. Katey later approached the Museum with the request that the time limit cover her own and Henry, her brother's death.

There were many unpleasant court cases over money in the family and in 1911 a large sum was raised "for the benefit of the descendents of Charles Dickens". The Daily Telegraph also opened a Christmas fund on their behalf in the columns of that newspaper, amounting to ten thousand pounds.

Mamie and Georgina went on to share a house with Henry where Ellen Ternan visited them when she later married.

With the passing of time, it was revealed that all the letters relating to the Dickens family had not been burnt at Gad's Hill. Georgina Hogarth learnt of a letter she had written which was coming onto the market in which she had stated Katey disliked a living person. When she learnt of this she asked Gladys Storey to procure the note so that it might be destroyed. The offending letter was purchased and together Katey and Gladys read it. Katey was "nettled" when she read that Georgina had called her "intolerant".

'"Aunty was not quite straight, and I often stood up to her; *that* is why she called me 'intolerant'".' When it came to her mother's letters, she said: '"you may keep them, do what you like with them, but do not read them to me – I could not bear it. My poor mother, would that I had been more kind to her. Letters! Letters! Letters! Never six months passes but letters crop up".' The note and other manuscripts were burnt in the fireplace as they sat there and Katey said it reminded her of the bonfire at Gad's Hill.

Watching the papers smoulder, a knock at the door brought another visitor, Lady Bell. Sitting down, she observed the pleasantries then said, "Kitty dear, we are not so well-off as we used to be, so I have sold some of your father's letters. I hope you don't mind?"

Katey looked at the embers in the grate turning to ashes. "'No – how strange".' When the caller had gone she instructed the maid there were to be no further visitors that day. As time passed she went on to say, "'I loved my father better than any man in the world – in a different way of course. I loved him for all his faults. My father was a wicked man – a very wicked man. My poor mother was afraid of my father. She was never allowed to express an opinion – never allowed to say what she felt". She then thought about her words. "We were *all* very wicked not to take her part; Henry does not take this view, but he was only a boy at the time, and does not realise the grief it was to our mother, after having all her children, to go away and leave us. My mother never rebuked me. I never saw her in a temper. "'We like to think of our geniuses as great characters – but we can't".'

Katey became ill and was increasingly beginning to see her mother's life in a different perspective. She bitterly regretted that she had not called in to see her on days she attended music lessons. Charles Alston had urged her to do so! She did think that if her mother were alive, she would not have been so surprised that the "Letters! Letters! Letters!" - were still turning up from time to time.

Recently a name, **Hector Charles Bulwer Lytton**

**Dickens** rose from the grave. It purported to be that of Georgina Hogarth's and Charles Dickens's son, born in Calcutta in 1854.

Does it fit into the jigsaw?

Hector, in his lifetime, became known as Charles Dickens the younger and stated the ring he proudly wore had been bought in 1890 from his allegedly, legitimate half brother Alfred Dickens, living in Australia and who had a need for money. On Hector's death the ring with letters, two wills and newspaper cuttings were passed on to his descendents but have now been sold at auction in England, being been bought by an anonymous buyer, thus the information the papers could have afforded have been kept out of the public domain – in effect, another burning.

It has been suggested that Hector could have been a conman, but it is difficult to see how such a man would have had the money to buy or access to the Dickens family. It seems more likely that a person longing to associate himself with his natural parents would be in a position to buy the artefact.

It is sad that the man Hector Charles Bulwer Lytton Dickens appears to have only inherited his name and that further pieces of the jigsaw have been prevented from being put in their place.

It is also interesting that Charles's descendents use the name Dickens between their forenames and surnames – it's a common practice and to me parallels the name of Hector.

A last look at the story is revealing. When Charles was a child he enquired. 'What is "your very best, the very best ale" a glass?' When advised of the cost his reply was, '"just draw me a glass of that, if you please, with a good head to it".'

He made no attempt to purchase the weaker half-beer version often drunk by children.

His wine cellar when sold off after his death contained two hundred dozen of the best wines, spirits and liqueurs, personally selected. These fetched six hundred and seventeen pounds, five shillings and eight pence.

## The Will.

The document opens with Ellen Ternan being left a legacy of £1,000 plus other financial considerations. His "dear sister-in-law Georgina Hogarth" received £8,000 plus jewellery and papers "and I leave her my grateful blessing as the best and truest friend man ever had". Charley inherited his father's library and pictures and Forster his gold watch and the manuscripts of his books.

In the same testament he told his children to remember how much they owed to Georgina, "I solemnly enjoin my dear children always to remember how much they owe to the said Georgina Hogarth, and never to be wanting in a grateful and affectionate attachment to her, for they know well that she has been, through all the stages of their growth and progress, their ever useful self-denying and devoted friend". The will went on "AND I DESIRE here simply to record the fact that my wife, since our separation by consent, has been in receipt from me of an annual income of £600, while all the great charges of a numerous and expensive family have devolved wholly upon myself"

## Burial.

It is ironical that a death mask was made of Charles when he had an aversion for such things. He directed that he was to lie in the graveyard at Shorne but instead was interred in Westminster Abbey. In his will he had said "I emphatically direct that I be buried in an inexpensive, un-ostentatious and strictly private manner….."

Regretfully, Charles's "Violated letter" and other writings tell more of himself than it does of Catherine and of his being a master of invalidation. Sadly, for Catherine in particular, their life together deepened into the Dickens tragedy for which Charles could find no resolution or ever reveal its many secrets.

The End

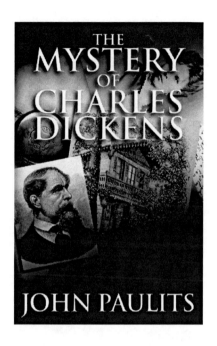

*"The book was a page turner. I was so sorry that it ended. Great character sketches drawn. There is a waiting list in The Dickens Fellowship in Boston to read this story (with its)... Dickensian master-plot. Such fine details expressed from the Palaces in Italy to the very wardrobe that Dickens wore. It was as if some one was following Charles and taking notes of all the goings on. A fast read and, of course, I could not put it down"* **Boston Dickens Fellowship**

Lightning Source UK Ltd.
Milton Keynes UK
UKOW031033030613

211675UK00001B/9/P